Contents

Acknowledgements

NIACE is very grateful to the Department for Education and Employment for their support to conduct this study.

A large number of people contributed information for the study and gave up their time to arrange field visits and meetings. My sincere thanks are due to all of the following:

Kate Basterfield, Stirchley Primary School

Beryl Bateson, Birmingham Education

Geoff Bateson, Core Skills Partnership

Steve Brunt, Karl Barton, Jenny Turner, John Chapman, Neil Ash, R K Britton, Jane Crispin, Wendy Poole, Ruth Ardron, Trudy Pankhurst Green, the Coalfields Learning Initiatives Partnership

Helen Butler, Voluntary Sector Training Group Northamptonshire

Elaine Capizzi, educational consultant

Liz Cousins, Fast Forward

Guy Farrar, Sharing Credit

Michael Freeston, National WEA

Alan Gale, Langold Community Resource Centre: Smokeys Sports and Social Club

Sue Georgious and Mari Lyall, Open College Network Central England

Lesley Haughton, Guidance consultant and Associate of the (National Institute for Careers Education and Counselling) NICEC

Jill Kibble, Celia Moorhouse, Hazel Greenwood, Margaret Shott, Park Lane College

Bronwen Maxwell, Welsh College of Horticulture.

Bryan Merton, NIACE

Margaret Morris, North Nottingham College

John McIntyre, University College of Technology, Sydney

John Popham, FE Europe

Les Price, Linwood Community Education Centre, Leicester

Margaret Prosser, Royal College of Dean College

Chris Rose, Birmingham City Council

Ken Simons, Norah Fry Research Centre

Jim Soulsby, NIACE

Ann Stamper NFWI

Jeannie Sutcliffe. NIACE

Alastair Thomson, NIACE

Alan Tuckett, NIACE

Cheryl Turner, NIACE

Stephanie Varah, Nottinghamshire County Council Community Services: Bassetlaw Community Development Team

Fran Walker, North Nottingham College

David Wilson, Northamptonshire LEA

Peter Wilson and Hazel Glover, National Open College Network

I would also like to thank Beryl Bateson, Jacqui Buffton and Pam Cole for their kind hospitality during some of the field trips.

Executive summary

1   Informal learning

1.1 Informal learning is difficult to pin down in an exact definition: it has been variously defined as unpremeditated or incidental learning; explicit learning which does not have a prescribed framework; learning which is informal in style and delivery but which includes a teacher and a structure. Some classify any form of non accredited adult education as informal.

1.2 Informal learning can be unpremeditated or self-directed, intentional and planned. It can be generated by individuals; it can be initiated by groups with a shared interest or concern; it can be initiated by outside agencies responding to community interests and needs or education providers who wish to offer previously excluded groups learning opportunities in their own environment.

1.3 It is difficult to make a clear distinction between informal and formal learning as there is often some crossover between the two. The setting is not necessarily a defining element: some informal learning takes place in formal educational environments while some formal learning takes place in informal local settings.

1.4 For the purposes of the study, informal learning was defined as:
- Learning that takes place outside a dedicated learning environment and which arises from the activities and interests of individuals or groups, but which may not be recognised as learning.
- Non course-based learning activities (which might include discussion, talks or presentations, information, advice and guidance) provided or facilitated in response to expressed interests and needs by people from a range of sectors and organisations (health, housing, social services, employment services, education and training services, guidance services).
- Planned and structured learning such as short courses organised in response to identified interests and needs but delivered in flexible and informal ways and in informal community settings.

2   Community settings

2.1 Informal learning takes place in a huge variety of settings. These may include dedicated learning environments such as community education centres and schools, but are often non educational settings such as village halls, community centres, clubs, voluntary groups, shopping centres or pubs. Voluntary organisations and community groups are significant providers of informal learning.

2.2 The location of learning is extremely important, often more so than its actual focus. This is due not only to practical but to psychological and cultural factors. In some areas it is found that people are very reluctant to participate in activities outside their familiar local environment.

2.3 Community-based informal learning plays a critical role in widening participation among

vi *Informal learning in the community*

people who are educationally, economically and socially disadvantaged. The people attracted to the informal learning provision profiled in this study were low income groups, long-term unemployed, people with no qualifications; lone parents, ethnic minority groups, those suffering from multiple deprivation (the homeless etc.)

2.4 It is difficult to estimate the exact amount of informal learning that is undertaken in community settings because of its scale and diversity and because it is often both a part and a product of ostensibly non educational activities. For the same reason it is difficult to measure its overall impact. However, there is substantial evidence that it can lead to important and mutually reinforcing benefits for learners.

3 Progression

3.1 In the context of adult learning, 'progression' can mean several things – personal progression, social progression, economic progression and educational progression. These frequently overlap.

3.2. Progression outcomes should not be too narrowly defined. What may be a small step for one person may be a huge distance to travel for another.

3.3 In all of the instances looked at in the course of this study, community-based learning had led to outcomes such as:
- Significantly increased self-confidence and self-esteem.
- Development of knowledge and understanding.
- Improved personal and social skills.
- New practical skills.
- Greater personal autonomy.

3.4 It had also motivated and helped many people to progress in one or several of the following ways:
- Changes in personal life and quality of life.
- Involvement in further learning in different places and at different levels.
- Wider involvement in the local community (more active citizenship).
- Movement into employment, self-employment or voluntary work.

The numbers of people taking these routes inevitably varied widely in different informal learning situations. In many cases, learners had progressed along several of these dimensions simultaneously.

3.5 Different types of informal learning produce slightly different patterns of progression. Informal learning generated by local people themselves often leads to wider community involvement and activism; learning arranged by education providers most often leads to high rates of educational progression; informal and incidental learning of the kind gained in voluntary organisations often leads to job acquisition, changes of career and wider involvement in the community. Most importantly, informal learning initiatives linked with community development and regeneration gives disadvantaged individuals and communities a route out of despair and depression.

3.6 Informal learning can result in important benefits not only for the individual but for the family and for the community or society as a whole. Many of the examples of informal learning seen in the course of the study were having an important 'ripple' or multiplier effect as social and familial networks in some excluded communities are very strong.

4 Educational progression

4.1 Informal learning often starts people with no qualifications or experience of post school education on a continuing learning path by helping them to become confident and successful learners.

4.2 Many of the individuals who engage in informal learning do not have educational progression as an aim and would not identify themselves as learners. In most of the cases profiled, 'onward and upward' progression to structured formal learning was unplanned and unanticipated. Very few of the people involved would have considered entering formal education programmes without prior engagement in informal learning. It was the positive learning experience in a familiar local environment that had stimulated new interests and enthusiasms and motivated people to continue learning.

4.3 Educational progression often follows a similar pattern despite the diversity of informal learning arrangements, activities and settings. People start learning informally for a variety of reasons often arising out of their immediate interests, priorities and concerns. Since much informal learning is embedded in non educational activities and does not take the form of a taught course, it is not always recognised as learning. During it, however, confidence grows and aspirations and expectations are widened. New interests and needs are identified and at this point learning often becomes conscious and explicit. At this stage learners are often ready to move on to more structured, learning activities. In order to do so, however, they need information, encouragement, coherent progression routes and support structures.

5 Factors that facilitate educational progression

5.1 The evidence indicates that the factors that enable people to continue learning are:

- The intervention and help of 'key' individuals who inform, motivate, enthuse, encourage and advise individuals and groups and act as intermediaries between them and education providers. These are not always education or guidance workers but can be health visitors, community workers, volunteers, pre-school playgroup leaders etc.

- Structures and services that enable progression (information and guidance services; inter-agency partnerships, Open College Networks, access networks, links between informal and formal providers).

- Flexible and responsive education/training providers and systems.

- Provision that responds to identified interests and needs and encourages progression by including confidence-building activities, planning for progression and processes to recognise achievements (e.g. portfolios, accreditation).

- Provision of both informal and more formal learning opportunities at the same site.

- Programmes designed to help people learn incrementally or make the transition from one type of learning to another (accredited programmes; Access courses, bridging courses, taster sessions, Return to Learn etc.)

- Strategies that enable progression between different learning levels (modular approaches, accreditation frameworks, APEL, articulation between outreach and mainstream provision).

- Support mechanisms that help people overcome any obstacles that might have prevented them from engaging in formal learning (help with finance, travel, childcare; provision of learning support in areas such as basic education, English language, study skills).

5.2 The first of these – key people – emerged as the most important factor in encouraging people to continue learning and to progress from informal to formal programmes. Without the support of local outreach and guidance workers or other people working in the community, many individuals would not have made the transition to formal education or training programmes. This highlights the importance of investing in development work in the community. Development work may be time-consuming and labour-intensive, with uncertain outcomes in the short-term, but the long-term results justify greater investment.

5.3. The study suggests that although educational progression is an important and desirable outcome of informal learning, first-step learning provision should be valued for itself rather than just as a route to more formal learning, qualifications and employment.

5.4 Too strong an emphasis on linear progression may undermine efforts to widen participation. Pre-determined standards such as those applied in qualification courses are incompatible with informal learning which is essentially flexible and responsive. Provision that is customised to the interests and requirements of new learners can have a greater and more positive impact on individuals and communities than the achievement of objectives set by providers or examining bodies.

5.5 The system of funding by outcomes does not take account of the fact that adult learning pathways are not always in a single direction. Adults, especially women, are more likely to follow an irregular, 'zig zag' educational trajectory than a linear one.

5.6 Although it is important to provide incremental learning opportunities and accreditation for all who want them, in some disadvantaged areas it would be unrealistic to expect immediate outcomes in the form of movement to progressively more advanced levels of learning. It can take a long time to raise the confidence and aspirations of multiply-deprived groups. For some such as the homeless, regular commitment to a learning programme is unlikely and learning groups are volatile.

6 Quality

6.1 It is important to find means other than accreditation for measuring value in informal education.

6.2 Quality indicators for informal education might relate to: a)the nature and character of the learning (objectives; content; the way it is set up, organised and delivered and the support structures provided); b)the achievements and results of the learning for those involved; c) the kind of 'exit' or continuation strategies provided for learners.

6.3 **Characteristics**

This study suggests that the most effective community-based learning is:

- Targeted at specific groups, especially those who are disadvantaged socially, economically and educationally.
- Offered in informal community venues.
- Offered at low cost or free of charge.
- Provided in response to consultation with learners.
- Tailored to group or individual needs, allowing people to set their own learning agendas;
- Flexible in terms of delivery and content and adaptable to the emerging interests and changing circumstances of learners.
- Offered with a range of support services that help to eliminate barriers to participation in learning.

These features make learning accessible to people with few qualifications who traditionally have not participated in post school education or training. They should all be considered as important indicators of quality.

6.4 **Objectives**

Another measure of quality should be the intentions of the learner. Most of the learning situations profiled in the study had been entered into intentionally with the objective of bringing about a desired change either for the individual, a family, a group, or for the community. Change can be something tangible, such as acquiring new skills and competences, or something subjective such as greater awareness and understanding.

6.5 Informal learning is often a collective rather than an individual process, with people coming together as a group and seeking ways of responding to local issues and problems. Learning that is entered into for the collective or community good should be also an indicator of quality.

6.6 **Outcomes**

Measures of quality should include the diverse outcomes of learning. Learners should be encouraged to define the objectives of their learning (an action plan); to reflect on their learning at regular intervals and to identify desired and other outcomes and the impact these have had on the individual, the immediate family or the wider community. This should make it possible to measure the extent to which informal learning meets the objectives of participants and to identify the overall range of outcomes (which are invariably much wider than original learning objectives).

6.7 Where possible, those providing informal learning should provide learners with guidance on continuation strategies and track their subsequent progression routes. These might include: making changes to personal life and life style; greater involvement in community activities; acquisition of jobs, career changes; self-employment; engagement in voluntary work; participation in other learning. None of these progression routes should be assigned a greater value than the others.

7. Although informal learning is the most widespread form of learning, until recently it has received little recognition and investment. Informal learning should be valued and supported for its own sake not just for its contribution to educational progression. It should not be transformed into something different by funding regimes and constraints related to targets. This would be counter-productive and deter many potential learners. It is precisely the flexibility, creativity and responsiveness of much informal learning that opens up to people the possibility of engaging in formal and accredited learning.

Introduction

Although the principles of lifelong learning are now widely accepted, education and training programmes provided in dedicated centres and institutions still attract only certain segments of the adult population. It is well established that this is due to a range of factors such as low self-confidence, poor previous educational experience, lack of awareness of opportunities, family and work commitments, inappropriate content and delivery, inability to meet costs, and problems with travelling to sites of learning.

Many people who experience these barriers nevertheless become involved in informal learning activities outside education institutions: *'within the activities they undertake as citizens, members of society, campaigners etc'* (Jackson, 1995). Informal learning can be far more effective than any recruitment or publicity strategy in encouraging people who do not habitually participate in education and training to embark on a learning pathway. For a long time this has been ignored. Coffield (1998), for example, notes that the debate about lifelong learning has become dominated by education and training providers despite the fact that informal learning is the main form of learning for many people.

Recently, however, there has been a revival of interest in informal learning in the community and recognition of its value both to individuals and to society, as evinced in *The Learning Age*:

> *Learning contributes to social cohesion and fosters a sense of belonging, responsibility and identity. In communities affected by rapid economic change and industrial restructuring, learning builds local capacity to respond to this change* (DfEE, 1998a)

This acknowledgement of the importance of community-based learning has been accompanied by new sources of support for local learning initiatives, among others, the Adult and Community Learning Fund, the National Lottery New Opportunities Fund, as well as a plethora of local partnerships to support widening participation and lifelong learning. These have strengthened the position of informal learning initiatives although there is still a huge gap between the resources allocated to the informal sector and those allocated to formal education and training. There is, nevertheless, considerable Government interest in the role of the sector in contributing to widening participation and community regeneration, as this and other current studies testify.

Aims and objectives

The focus of this study was progression routes from informal learning in community settings. The principal aims were to investigate the extent to which informal learning helps people to progress in educational and other ways and how the process can be enabled and facilitated. The objectives were:

- To identify the range of contexts in which informal learning takes place, the nature of that learning and the kinds of people involved.
- To identify the routes that people can take from informal learning in community settings to other education and training programmes.
- To identify motives for educational progression and the kind of outcomes achieved by learners.
- To examine the extent to which progression routes in different types of community settings are linked to local infrastructures of education and training provision, access and accreditation networks and national qualification frameworks.
- To identify the factors and conditions that foster the development of learning pathways from informal learning and those which inhibit it.
- To identify the support needs of those wishing to progress from informal learning to more formal accredited or unaccredited education and training programmes.
- To consider how informal education in community settings can contribute to national agendas such as lifelong learning, widening participation, combating social exclusion.

Methods

The study was conducted between September 1998 and January 1999. Given the diversity of community settings in which informal learning activities take place, it was largely qualitative. It comprised three strands: a literature search, consultation with relevant agencies and individuals, and visits to informal learning environments and organisations providing informal learning in the community.

The literature search drew on previous studies undertaken for NIACE and existing research into informal learning and progression routes. The consultation element involved visits to, and communication by correspondence and telephone with, relevant agencies and organisations. The fieldwork entailed visits to groups and organisations involved in providing or facilitating informal learning in community venues. Where possible, meetings were also held with informal learners.

Because of the short time-scale for the project it was decided to use the time available to look at examples of informal learning that had been entered into intentionally by learners. The field visits focused on:

- The kinds of informal learning engaged in by adults.
- The target groups involved.
- The nature of links and partnership arrangements with education providers and other agencies.
- The funding sources used for informal learning and progression routes.
- The information and advice on other learning activities offered.
- The strategies and mechanisms encouraging progression.
- The outcomes for learners.

Visits were made to Langold Community Resource centre at Smokey's Sports and Leisure Club in Bassetlaw; North Nottinghamshire College; the Birmingham Inspire initiative and Cotsgrove and Stirchley junior schools; Royal Forest of Dean College; Park Lane College learning centre at Crossgates shopping centre, Leeds; Northern College (the Coalfields Learning Initiatives Partnership); Fast Forward (Nottinghamshire); the National WEA and the National Open College Network. Discussions were held with a representative of Birmingham Core Skills Partnership and an associate of the National Institute for Careers Education and Counselling (NICEC). Contact by correspondence and phone was also made with people connected with the National Federation of Women's Institutes, the Drome scheme in

Flintshire and a range of small voluntary groups and organisations. A list of all who assisted with the study is given in the Acknowledgement section.

The report
The report has been structured in the following way:

Section 1 considers definitions of informal learning and progression and the role of informal learning in widening participation.
Section 2 considers the various factors and conditions that assist educational progression.
Section 3 considers the factors that impede educational progression.
Section 4 summarises the findings, considers arguments for supporting informal learning and lists some points to be taken into consideration by policy makers and education and training providers.

The examples and case studies used in the report have been taken both from the fieldwork and previous research. These have not been included in a separate section but have been dispersed throughout the report to illustrate particular points.

It should be noted that although the study was supported by the DfEE, all observations, conclusions and recommendations are the author's own.

Concepts and definitions

Informal learning

There is no single definition of informal learning. It is a broad and loose concept that incorporates very diverse kinds of learning, learning styles and learning arrangements. Informal learning can be unpremeditated, self-directed, intentional and planned. It can be initiated by individuals (for example in the home, in the workplace); it can be a collective process (arising from grassroots community action or social protest), or it can be initiated by outside agencies responding to perceived or expressed needs, interests or problems. These may include education providers who wish to offer previously excluded groups learning experiences in their own environment.

It is difficult to make a clear distinction between informal and formal learning as there is often some crossover between the two. The setting itself is not necessarily a defining element: some informal learning takes place in formal educational environments (such as schools) while some formal learning takes place in an informal local setting (such as church or village halls).

Some analysts have tried to pin down the differences. Eraut *et al* (1998) draw a distinction between formal education and training which they define as having a prescribed framework for learning, and non formal learning which they define as explicit learning which is not constrained or supported by prescribed frameworks. This includes both self-directed learning which is essentially deliberate and reactive learning which is not pre-planned.

Other analysts differentiate between *non* formal learning where a learning process is initiated and controlled by learners and not always structured, and informal learning which can be independent and incidental but may also include a teacher and a structure. Some categorise as *non* formal any learning that is uncertificated, flexible, client-centred, short-term, responsive to needs and organised, taught and delivered in local settings and in informal ways. Simkins (1977) proposed that the three main features and advantages of such programmes were their low cost, relevance and flexibility. Fordham (1979) considered learner-centredness, flexibility and relevance to be paramount. He approved of a definition used in a Government of India pamphlet: '*Non formal education is life, environment and learner oriented. It is diversified in content and method; it is built on learner participation*'.

In recent times there has been a tendency (fallacious in the author's view) to make a simple distinction between accredited programmes which are considered to be formal and non-accredited programmes which are generally classified as informal. This discounts the wide variety of content, teaching and learning styles that can be found within both accredited and non-accredited education and training.

For the purposes of the study, informal learning has been defined as:

• Learning that takes place outside a dedicated learning environment, which arises from the activities and interests of individuals or groups but which may not be recognised as learning

(learning by doing, listening, observing, interacting with others, and so on).

- Non-course-based but intentional learning activities (which might include discussion, talks or presentations, information, advice and guidance) provided or facilitated in response to expressed interests and needs by people from a range of sectors and organisations (health, housing, social services, employment services, education and training services, guidance services).

Both of these kinds of learning often have as their starting point matters of immediate interest or concern to participants. Both can lead to:

- More structured, planned learning (short courses, etc.) organised in response to identified interests and needs but delivered in flexible and informal ways and in informal community settings.

The study was more concerned with learning for a purpose (even when not recognised as learning) than with incidental or passive informal learning (for example, through reading newspapers or watching television).

Community education

The terms non formal and informal education are sometimes used interchangeably with 'community education' – a catch-all term which also lacks an accepted definition and which is increasingly being replaced by other terms such as lifelong learning. The word 'community' has become contentious in recent years for reasons that were summed up by Martin (1987). He described 'community as a: *notoriously slippery and contested concept'* which was being applied increasingly ambiguously to:

> *a dubious assortment of localised relatively cheap and expediently ad hoc responses to fundamentally structural problems as education and the social services have been squeezed in the vice of an increasingly narrowly conceived economic policy.* (Martin, 1987: 12-13)

Other analysts have also advised that the word 'community' be used with care. One report described it as a term that is rarely defined but often used with scant regard for its range of potential meanings. The report distinguished between :

- *Geographical communities* which can vary in size from a street to a nation.
- *Occupational communities* composed of people working in similar fields, often across a very broad geographical area. These have common interests and can develop into closed and very powerful groups, some of which have a loyalty to a national rather than a local community.
- *Interest communities* composed of people sharing a common interest (e.g. clubs, societies, political parties).
- *Cultural communities* which may be based on origin, as in ethnic communities, or on common circumstances, as in working-class communities. *'Both may exist as very separate entities within a broader geographical area'.*

> *Most people are members of several of these communities and some will be better organised and more effective in expressing their needs than others. Interests will conflict, and any attempt to make a service accountable to a 'community' will need to be very clear about which community is intended.* (UDACE, 1987: 17)

When applied to education, however, the word 'community' generally suggests something that is desirable, accessible, locally-based and open to all. It also implies an approach that is cross-sectoral and more holistic than formal education: one which involves a: *'blurring of boundaries between educational establishments and their surrounding communities, as well as between teachers and students, work and leisure'* (Caudry, 1985). These are features common to much informal education in community settings. Other characteristics shared by informal learning and community education, as they are often understood, are that they are usually:

- Offered in informal local venues not in education institutions.
- Low cost or free of charge.
- Negotiated with learners.
- Tailored to group or individual needs.
- Offered with a range of support services.
- Attractive to people who traditionally have not participated in post-school education or training and those with few qualifications.

These features characterise all of the examples of informal learning visited during the course of this study.

Community settings

In the context of this study, the term 'community settings' is understood to mean a familiar local environment as distinct from a formal learning institution such as a further education college: any place where people gather in the course of their everyday lives – homes, shopping centres, village halls, community centres, churches, schools, playgroups, pubs and clubs. Primary schools may also be considered as community setting as these are familiar local environments and often the centre of local life in small communities and rural environments

Community settings also include the meeting places of local groups and voluntary organisations set up for a variety of purposes. In most residential areas there is a range of groups and organisations engaged in social, leisure, sports and voluntary activities although the nature and range of these depend on the economic and social characteristics of the district and the extent to which it is provided with services and facilities such as schools, community centres, places of worship, sports facilities, public houses etc. A Home Office working group (1998) has estimated that, nationally, there are *'hundreds of thousands'* of community groups (associations of people who come together to pursue a common cause or interest, often on a mutual basis, and usually run by volunteers for people like themselves). A study of local voluntary organisations (Elsdon, 1995) revealed an *'astonishing variety'*, from small sports clubs, discussion groups and arts organisations to self-help groups, social service organisations and local branches of national and wider organisations. Elsdon extrapolated from a survey in one geographical area (Retford) that there could be up to 1.3 million local voluntary organisations (LVOs) with over half of the adult population in membership.

Voluntary organisations perform a wide range of functions. Charnley, Osborn and Withnall (1981) found the most common were those concerned with:

- Charitable, religious and welfare concerns.
- Self-help and support for people affected by specific illnesses or addictions.
- Housing and the local environment.
- Commercial, industrial and professional activities and interests.

- Cultural interests (music, theatre, art, etc.)
- Recreation and specific interest.
- Sports.
- Political activities and issues.
- Social activities.
- The needs and concerns of specific groups (the elderly, widows, minority ethnic groups, parents, people with physical or learning disabilities, carers).
- Activities relating to a specific cause or interest (such as animal rights, the environment).

Another study (Kendall and Knapp, 1993) distinguished between organisations with a *service-providing* function (supplying a direct service to people in kind or in the form of information, advice and support); those with a *mutual aid function* (self-help and exchange around a common need or interest); those with a *pressure-group function,* and those with a *resource and co-ordinating function* (such as the National Council for Voluntary Organisations, the Charities Aid Foundation, the Volunteer Centre UK, and SIA – the national development agency for black voluntary and community organisations). All of these functions incorporate important elements of learning.

Learning in voluntary and community groups

Voluntary groups and organisations are significant providers of education and training. A paper prepared for the National Advisory Group on Continuing Education and Lifelong Learning refers to the *'vast range of learning activity'* that is conducted within the voluntary and community sector:

> *Relate and the Samaritans are just two examples of national voluntary bodies which equip their volunteers with useful new skills and which find the investment rewarded by an increased commitment to the agency and, through the agency, much greater practical benefit to the wider society. At local neighbourhood level the same processes are going on – albeit in much more informal and unstructured ways.* (Nolan *et al*, 1998)

Most voluntary organisations (especially the larger ones) provide some forms of education and training relevant to their specific goals and specialisms. Percy's (1988) study of a range of voluntary organisations typically found that they included elements of both formal learning (teaching, discussion, assessment and certification) as well as informal learning (practice learning, learning from other members, learning from experience and learning though social interaction).

An earlier study of voluntary organisations in Birkenhead (Elsey, 1974) investigated the activities of, among others, the Townswomen's Guild; the Eighteen Plus group; the Cage Bird Fanciers and the Homing Pigeons Society; the Model Railway and Model Boat Clubs, the Photographic Club; Choral Societies; Band and Drama groups and St. John's Ambulance. The study showed that, in varying degrees, all these organisations provided conventional educational activities such as organised programmes, instruction or teaching in the form of lectures, talks or advice from experts. Some also included other activities with an educational element – quizzes, question and answer panels and public demonstrations of knowledge and skills such as exhibitions and stage performances.

A more recent survey of voluntary groups in Northamptonshire (1998) also found a considerable amount of planned learning activities in the groups surveyed, including talks, demonstrations, visits, social and musical activities and religious studies.

Groups set up to serve particular sections of the community often routinely incorporate learning in their activities. The National Federation of Women's Institutes (NFWI), for example, offers a wide range of informal and formal courses for women in rural areas. There are now 20 lifelong learning centres based in federations' headquarters and the NFWI also has a residential centre, Denman College, which offers short residential courses, some with accreditation. The college was used by over 6,000 students in 1997-98.

Community-based groups for pre-school-aged children also provide learning opportunities for adults. The Pre-School Learning Alliance, for example, offers parents and carers a range of courses in areas such as learning through play, child development and pre-school practice.

Many organisations for people with disabilities or learning difficulties include learning in their activities. In Brighton, Care Coops, a voluntary group, involves people with learning difficulties in photography, IT, art and making videos. It also engages members in the running of a community farm which produces organic vegetables.

Organisations, groups or movements that focus on everyday concerns such as health, housing and finance also habitually provide some elements of education or training for their members. For example self-help or advisory groups set up for people affected by particular diseases or substance abuse automatically include a strong element of learning. Similarly, housing associations and co-operatives involve learning activities and often help members to develop transferable knowledge and skills:

> *In housing co-operatives education is particularly important since they demand a high commitment and skill among the average members and members exercise responsibility often for several million pounds of housing stock. Education also aims to develop team-working communication, accountability to all tenant members and the building up of the wider community.*
> (Fazaeli, 1991: 23)

Some housing projects provide practical learning activities for specific groups. One example is Swallow, a small housing project in Radstock which has members with learning difficulties. The project has organised a research fieldwork trip to look at services in France and has also encouraged members to make their own video about the project. Another example is the African Refugee Housing Action Group (ARHAG), a housing association in London which offers skills training and help with job search and setting up small business ventures.

Local credit unions also provide learning opportunities. There are over 600 registered credit unions in Britain and one of their aims is to educate members in the use of money and management of financial affairs:

> *The volunteering involves committee work, book-keeping, computer skills, presentations, campaigning, consulting, collective decision-making, negotiating, crisis management, minute-taking and member relations. All of these are skills that enhance self-esteem and are transferable to other organisations or to employment.* (Macfarlane, 1997: 52)

A study conducted a few years ago found that much of the training for credit union volunteers was 'rather informal and of the hands-on type' but that more formal training sessions in areas such as book-keeping, managerial skills and the role of cashiers, treasurers and board members, were also held on a regular basis using group work, role play and question and answer sessions (Weller, 1993).

Sometimes several voluntary groups work together in developing or brokering learning opportunities for a particular section of the community. ACTIVE (Association of Community Training Initiatives for Vocational Education) in central Birmingham – a consortium composed of organisations representing the black and Asian communities in Handsworth and Lozells – was established to provide advice, support and training to unemployed people.

Unplanned learning

Despite these examples of explicit educational activity, much and perhaps most of the learning that goes on in voluntary organisations is unplanned and incidental and therefore neither described nor recognised as learning.

Elsdon's (1995) study of local voluntary groups and organisations (LVOs) revealed:

> *a great range of learning, change and satisfaction over and above those which are deliberate, inherent in the organisation's objectives and expected by their members (. . .) an astonishing range and intensity of learning, attitudinal change and development is fermenting in most LVOs in addition to whatever is assumed to be their range of activities. (. . .) Rather than 'unintended' this is unpremeditated learning, an uncovenanted access (. . .) All groups mediated at least some deliberate learning (that which objectives promised). The significant finding is that all mediated at least some unpremeditated learning and change.*
> (Elsdon, 1995: 47-49)

In Australia, according to a new study, women's neighbourhood centres can be seen as: '*sites of leaning, arenas in which significant informal learning occurs. This learning is frequently tacit or implicit, embedded as it is in the routine activities of the centres*' (Foley, 1999). The same study demonstrates how social protest can be a potent instigator of informal learning leading to the development of organisational skills, social skills and communication skills as well as to a deeper critical understanding of society, group empowerment and knowledge. However, this process is not recognised or articulated as learning because: '*it is largely informal and often incidental: it is tacit, embedded in action and often not recognised as learning.*'

Similar findings have been reported in relation to the workplace. One study has found that a significant proportion of workplace learning is informal and unintentional and embedded in the work situation:

> *Our research shows how strongly [informal learning] is situated in the work itself and in its social and organisational context (. . .) Learning at work more often results as a by-product of the pursuit of work goals than from the pursuit of learning goals per se.* (Eraut, 1998: 26-27)

It is impossible to estimate the exact amount of informal learning that goes on in community and workplace settings, partly because of its sheer diversity and partly because it is often both a part and a product of ostensibly non-educational activities.

Informal learners

The people who engage in informal learning include virtually everybody if one takes the broadest possible view of learning. However, the evidence suggests that informal learning in the community provides a particularly important learning starting point for women, people in manual occupations and low income groups, minority ethnic groups, people who are geographically or socially isolated, those who left school at an early age, and all who, for a range of reasons, would not consider formal education as appropriate or relevant to them:

> *Those individuals who feel themselves disenfranchised or excluded in the larger political sphere*

often gain their first stake by joining an ethnic association, or a single issue campaign, or by working with others to create alternative structures to reflect their own community's needs.
(Nolan *et al*, 1998)

It is commonly found that many women engage in informal learning when their children join local playgroups or schools. Many adult members of ethnic community groups also start on a learning pathway, informally, within their local communities (Ward, 1998). Such findings are not confined to Britain. In New Zealand, learning located in the local community has been found to be an essential re-entry point both for women and for Maori communities (Harre Hindmarsh and Davies, 1995).

British studies consistently show that a large number of individuals who return to learn informally in the community left school at an early age with few or no qualifications. In Elsey's study of voluntary organisations (1974), for example, 43 per cent of all respondents had left school early and few had subsequently engaged in any form of organised education. Elsdon's study (1995) showed that even local organisations concerned with the arts, academic study and general education attracted: *'a significantly higher proportion of people with an early school leaving age than would have been expected'.* This, taken together with Elsdon's estimate that about half of the adult population are involved in local voluntary organisations, suggests that locally-based learning has a huge potential role in widening participation in education and training.

Progression

In the context of adult learning the term 'progression' can mean a number of things. Participation in learning can lead to *personal* progression (greater confidence, autonomy and self-esteem; broader understanding, improved literacy); *social* progression (better mixer, wider network, greater community participation) and *economic* progression (acquisition of jobs), as well as to *educational* and academic progression (FEDA, 1997). Although it is useful to think of these as separate processes, as Percy and Ward (1991) have pointed out, they frequently overlap and are inter-related. Surveys of learners (for example, Maxwell, 1997) have revealed that many learners progress along several of these dimensions simultaneously.

Informal learning appears to lead to these outcomes because of its ability to raise levels of confidence and self-esteem. A study of informal learning in the workplace found that :

Confidence encouraged more ambitious goal-setting and more risk-taking, both leading to further learning usually relating to the ability to execute a task or successfully perform a role.
(Eraut, 1998: 26-27)

Other studies have demonstrated that, for many people, informal learning in the community is a potent catalyst for change and personal development. Elsdon (1995) found that individuals involved in local voluntary organisations had acquired a wide range of skills and personal attributes which they were able to transfer to their lives beyond the group. These included social and interpersonal skills, knowledge and skills relating to the respective organisation; skills and aptitudes that assisted their performance, standing or development in their current job, wider political understanding, and skills they could use in their personal lives. His study indicated that membership of local groups and organisations had helped *'an encouraging number'* of previously unqualified adults to enter the labour market as a result of their increased confidence and skills:

Competence, confidence, interpersonal and organising skills and readiness to discharge responsibility make people better at almost any job. They also alter the persona they present to other people; they become more impressive as well as more effective. Respondents gave numerous examples of such skills and attitudes which had eased or indeed enhanced their performance at work, but the key word which was mentioned almost invariably was confidence: it was the confidence acquired through membership of the LVO which had enabled the skills and attitudes to develop, or to be deployed. Responsibility with the LVO invariably meant planning, organising, ability to discuss and to listen, to tolerate disagreement and to stand up for one's own point of view. More generic skills learned in organisations were systematic policy-making and long-term planning and organisation and study (. . .)

Members of self-help groups learned skills such as systematic organisation which prepared them for the problems they were going to face (. . .) Perhaps the commonest experience (. . .) was that of people who had learned organising, managerial and negotiating skills as officers and members of committees and who took them from the LVO to all forms of paid work and to elected office. (Elsdon, 1995: 67)

Research into the outcomes for parents and carers using pre schools affiliated to the Pre-School Learning Alliance (PSLA) produced similar findings (McGivney, 1998b). That study showed that the involvement of users in the running of pre-schools had provided many with transferable knowledge and skills. Those who were actively involved in management committees as chairs, secretaries or treasurers had improved their social and communication skills and become effective team-workers. Some had become adept at dealing with external agencies such as Social Services. Many had also developed practical skills such as chairing meetings, taking minutes, keeping accounts, record-keeping, fund-raising and dealing with issues to do with insurance, staff pay, hire of premises, health and safety and legislation such as the Children Act. The acquisition of such skills had significantly increased confidence levels, as a result of which some women had obtained or changed employment. A significant number had gone on to join other local organisations and voluntary groups. Some had become play leaders and had started their own nurseries or play groups; others had become parent governors and officers in parish councils, local voluntary groups and parent-teacher associations.

There were also examples of educational progression. A fifth of respondents had been motivated to attend structured education and training courses provided by the Alliance. In some pre-schools, users who had not previously engaged in adult education had attended as many as twelve PSLA courses and some had subsequently gone on to take higher level education and training courses elsewhere. Several had embarked upon teacher-training courses, a direction that they had never previously considered taking (McGivney, 1998b).

Educational progression

This study was primarily concerned with the extent to which informal learning leads to more systematic and intentional learning and the kinds of factors that assist in this process. This does not mean that educational progression is the most important outcome of informal learning or that transition to a more advanced or demanding course or programme is the *only* form of educational progression, although it has inevitably acquired this meaning. Depending on the interests, needs and circumstances of the learner, educational progression can be in a sideways and downwards direction as well as outwards and upwards: a move to another learning programme at the same level in the same or a different subject area, or a move to a lower learning level:

Adult learners often switch levels of learning in a way that challenges our traditional ideas of progress. They are also remarkably promiscuous in their learning, ranging from subject to subject in a remarkable way. (Ball, 1999)

Research indicates that adult learning patterns vary according to age, gender and race. A study conducted in New Zealand (Harre Hindmarsh and Davies, 1995) examined the extent to which non-formal learning in the Wellington region was the starting point of a pathway into education and training opportunities in other sectors. Interviews with learners (which included many women and members of Maori communities) revealed three dominant patterns. Individuals were:

- moving backwards and forwards between formal and non formal learning opportunities (a zig-zag pattern).
- moving from non formal to formal learning (a linear pattern), or:
- moving between different non formal learning programmes (a cyclic pattern).

The study suggested that over the whole lifespan, adult learning pathways were likely to be characterised by a zig-zag pattern. However, different groups had different patterns. Younger adults tended to have a linear learning pathway while those in their middle or later years, and those committed to caring for dependents for extended periods, followed a more zig-zag route. Women tended to have more of a cyclic pattern than men, and those improving their basic education or seeking qualifications also followed a more extended cyclic than a linear pathway. Communities intent on advancing economically (such as ethnic groups) encouraged a linear learning pattern among their members.

Nearer to home, a study conducted in Wales (Maxwell, 1997) also found different progression patterns relating to age and gender. The study investigated the destinations of learners who had participated in the *Drome* learning programme. It revealed that learners aged 26 to 45 were more likely to progress to other education opportunities, to gain or change employment or to take on voluntary work than learners of other ages, and that men were significantly more likely than women to join a local hobby or interest group after participation. Women were more likely than men to move into both uncertificated courses and GCSE and A Levels. Men were more likely than women to take only one further learning activity, whereas women were more likely than men to progress to two or more further learning activities.

Such findings indicate that definitions of 'progression' need to take account of adult characteristics and life situations since these strongly influence patterns of engagement in learning. Accordingly, a succession of studies and reports have stressed that learner progression can be both lateral and vertical and that one should not necessarily assign a higher value to the latter as has tended to happen since the introduction of the concept of 'levels'.

Progression is not always linear. Students do not necessarily start in one class and progress smoothly to another. Some jump directly into more formally organised advanced classes (...) and others might never progress past general literacy classes. (...) People should have choices: moving sideways, staying out or progressing forwards. The problem is when there's nowhere to go. (Temple, 1991: 25-26)

For many adults 'progression' involves pursuing the same sorts of courses in the same sorts of settings; pursuing different sorts of courses while staying in the same setting; pursuing different (rather than more advanced) modules or degrees in further and higher education. For many adults

2 The role of informal learning in widening participation and starting people on a learning pathway

The starting point for this study was the belief that informal learning in community settings constitutes the beginning of a learning pathway for a great many people, as well as helping them to progress in other dimensions of their lives. To test this belief, an extensive literature search was conducted and a number of visits were made to a range of locations where informal learning takes place. These included:

- outreach locations used by formal institutions.
- a 'shop and learn' complex.
- a regional scheme for community development and regeneration.
- a resource and leisure centre.
- a community centre involved in providing community support, advice and education.
- an adult residential college.
- two junior schools.

The evidence from the visits confirmed the findings of previous research in showing that informal learning in community settings plays a critical role in widening participation and starting people off on a learning path. As one informant working in a very disadvantaged area testified: *'Once started they're hooked. Everyone here has gone on to something else. Once started you can't stop them.'*

The process

Despite the diversity of informal learning situations and settings, participation in locally-based learning often follows a similar pattern, as examples in this and the following sections demonstrate.

It is often a collective rather than an individual process. People come together because of shared interests and concerns or because a structure exists that enables a group to form (a crèche, a playgroup, a parents' group, a tenants' association, a church, etc.). The group, sometimes with the help of those working with them, identify common information or skill needs and at this point, 'key' people such as group leaders, community workers, education development workers, health workers or volunteers step in to provide relevant information or bring in outside experts to engage in discussion with members of the group. This often leads to informal learning activities – demonstrations, group activities, action research, visits, discussion groups – which frequently stimulate people to continue learning. According to a community outreach worker:

People come and participate in informal learning for a multiplicity of reasons. These will usually be collective reasons. As you go through the process there will be learning outcomes and a whole host of possibilities arise. We need to capitalise on this.

He gave the following example which illustrates the process:

The Linwood Community Education Centre on the Saffron Estate in Leicester is an area with three times the national average of lone parents and a higher than average proportion of families with three or more children under nine. Many families on the estate receive housing benefit and over 50 per cent of the children are eligible for free school meals. 95 per cent of residents left school at an early age and there are high levels of economic inactivity. Among the children there is significant underachievement at key stages 1-3 and GCSE. At the same time the estate has *'a vigorous social economy, strong kinship and familial links and active community networks'*.

Some years ago, tenants who were worried about the implications of local development plans approached community education workers for advice. An informal education programme was subsequently set up, the starting points for which were the questions: *what do we already know and what do we need to know?* A regular learning group met to explore relevant issues with the help of outside speakers such as local politicians and representatives from the local authority and housing association. Although the group numbered about 15, there was: *'an active periphery of about 80. The small groups passed on their learning and we got feedback from a much wider group. We were servicing a network rather than a defined group of learners'*.

Key factors that stimulated the initial learning process were:
- It arose out of identified needs and concerns. Local people themselves decided what they needed to know
- It was organised in a way that built organically on what was happening in the community.

According to the community education worker: *'a whole host of learning opportunities spiralled out of those initial pragmatic goals'*. They led, for example, to an interest in local history and local research which resulted in residents writing and publishing a book on the history of the Saffron Estate: *'This was a learning outcome that came directly out of the process. You can't systematise that. Informal learning uncovers myriad possibilities'*.

(Information supplied by Les Price, the Linwood Centre)

In this example, the informal learning process was generated largely by local people in an attempt to understand and influence a local situation. What they learned was swiftly passed on to the wider community. According to the community education worker:

> There are a lot of misconceptions about informal learning. A lot of it is collective. It's not just the group that are ostensibly involved. It operates by a cascade process. Information is passed on and cascades out into the community. There are organic networks and if informal learning can tap into these you can achieve far more than with those you meet on a regular basis. You can have a major impact in terms of social stability with a piece of learning that involves eight people. The key is to use kinship or wider family networks, and train people to disseminate information in forms that are easily replicable.

In the next example, the learning process came about as the result of two disparate groups, residents and health professionals, having different perspectives on a problem that both had an interest in solving.

Another example of collective learning on the Saffron Estate was the **Parent Peer Group Programme**. This developed after an outbreak of head lice in local schools generated anxieties about social stigma. Health professionals – health visitors and doctors – had other concerns, namely the over-use of pesticides, and they wanted people to use other methods to manage the problem. A two-way learning process ensued: health visitors who visited parents learnt from them that there was a strong social dimension to a problem they had previously seen as purely technical. At the same time parents discovered a way of dealing with the problem which did not involve pesticides. A cascade training programme was subsequently set up for parents, with the assistance of community education workers, showing them how to demonstrate the wet-combing method to others on the estate: *'part of our role is to try and act as a catalyst and facilitator for that collective process.'* (Information supplied by Les Price, the Linwood Centre)

In the following example, it is the community venue that has been instrumental in bringing back into learning many people with little or no post school education experience and few qualifications. The key factor is the siting, in a local working men's club, of an information and support centre for local people, staffed by volunteers. As well as advice, the centre offers a range of learning opportunities in response to community interests. Here, as is often the case, people come for one purpose and stay for another.

Langold Community Resource Centre, located until recently in Smokey's Sports and Leisure club in Bassetlaw, operates as a drop-in social and support centre for local people. It is run by a voluntary committee with co-opted representatives from Nottinghamshire County Council, Bassetlaw Community Development Team and North Nottinghamshire College. At the time of visit there were 19 volunteers all of whom were keeping portfolios which were regularly updated.

The centre offers:
- Advice on welfare and benefit rights.
- Information on local education and training opportunities.
- Business advice from Nottinghamshire County Council and the Prince's Youth Trust.
- Careers advice for people under 19.
- Adult careers advice. (The centre keeps regularly updated databases containing details of local job vacancies and all advertised jobs within Nottinghamshire and surrounding counties. Job seekers are able to use the centre's stationery, phone, fax and computers for CV preparation and job enquiries.
- Additional off-site support (for example, people can borrow laptop computers to use at home).
- A range of informal and accredited courses.
- Childcare facilities.
- A meeting place for local community groups.

The centre has received funding on an annual basis from a range of sources including Nottinghamshire County Council Economic Development Section and Community Services Council. Additional support comes from the Welfare Rights Service, North Nottinghamshire TEC, Bassetlaw District Agency and Bassetlaw Community Development Team. It also receives financial support from the *Fast Forward* county-wide scheme to mount a range of unaccredited and accredited courses delivered by a range of providers.

The aim of the centre (which has won a national award for Reaching-Out Services in the Community) is to respond to local needs and help people build their self-confidence. Where necessary, people are referred to other agencies: *'The philosophy we follow is "we are here to help you help yourself, and if we don't know we will find someone who does"'*.

All learning and support activities at the centre are in response to expressed interests and needs. Providers include North Nottinghamshire College, the WEA, the Red Cross and the Coal Industry Social Welfare Organisation. In Autumn 1998, courses were offered in computing up to RSA Level 2 (the centre is an RSA accredited Examination Centre),word processing, sign language, basic English, first aid at work, health and safety and food hygiene. Learner achievements are celebrated several times during the year.

The centre is popular and well-used. In 1998 there were about 300 registered users, most of them residents of disadvantaged local wards and estates: *'for some long-term unemployed men, coming to Langold is the only thing that will get them out of bed in the daytime'*. It is clearly a place in which people feel comfortable and relaxed. When visited (at around 3pm on a weekday) there were people who had dropped in on a social basis; volunteers doing various tasks; a group working on laptops with a tutor and another group (mainly middle-aged men) learning German. A man with learning difficulties was working at a computer. He has developed a certain expertise and has helped to develop the centre's website. In the church hall that serves as an annexe, several young men were getting their musical instruments ready for a forthcoming event.

Few and probably none of the people engaged in learning had previously considered approaching an education institution. They had usually visited the resource centre for another purpose (advice on welfare rights; help with job search), had found it a helpful and congenial environment and had gradually become involved in a wider range of activities including learning. Many had also become active as volunteers.

The volunteers keep track of users and note their destinations. They are proud of the fact that in 1997, 23 long-term unemployed people found jobs and two ex-miners had enrolled in teacher training courses as a direct result of the support and learning activities provided at the centre. These are considered huge achievements for this former mining area.

Users of the centre
A, the chairman of the voluntary management committee, is an ex-forces regular who was made redundant from a management position in Sheffield several years ago. He became involved in the centre at its inception and has worked without pay since then to make it a self-sufficient, well managed community facility. Through this work he has gained a range of new skills and developed his existing skills.

B, who is on long-term sick leave, has been a member of Langold Community Resource Centre since 1995: *'It took me a good three months to actually come through the door of the Resource Centre. However with the help of volunteers my fears diminished'*. She eventually became a volunteer and a member of the management committee where her current role is to keep the monthly statistics in order. She enjoys her role and tries: *'to help anyone I can'*. She has participated in several courses since she started coming to the centre – Introduction to using a computer, RSA CLAIT Level 1, desktop publishing, using and designing a database level 2, and FE Award, Level 2. She has also taken courses in basic food hygiene and is the Centre's appointed First Aid person.

C has been coming to centre for about three years, during the course of which he has become involved in some of the learning opportunities provided. He has taken courses in first aid, counselling, computers, maths and English. He is now starting a second level course in computers and one in sign language. He has recently become a volunteer as: *'I like to help and have made loads of friends'.* The counselling course helped him to become a Samaritan.

D became involved in the centre after he was made redundant. He gradually became involved in learning and has participated in courses in computing, counselling, communication skills and caring, *'all of which help me to help others, and of course myself.'* He was invited to serve on the management committee in 1997 and is now the treasurer. He has also served on the Parish Council and has been a school governor.

E has been unemployed for over six months and has been a volunteer at the centre for four months: *'I first learnt about it a year ago and have now got involved in the Internet. I'm designing a Web Page for the Centre and it will be up and running soon. I have done two courses on a web designing course'.*

F, who is employed part-time, has been a volunteer at the centre for over five years. She has found it an invaluable resource in helping people gain their confidence and providing them with advice on issues such as welfare rights. Since becoming involved she has participated in a range of learning activities including courses in first aid, introduction to computers, RSA CLAIT Level 1 and childcare. In the last few years she has become a leader of the Brownies and secretary of a local charity event, both of which she ascribes to her involvement in the centre: *'without the support of the centre I would have not been able to achieve any of it'.*

G has been using the centre for three years and has been a volunteer for over two. She has taken courses in first aid, GCSE Maths, RSA CLAIT Level 1 and desktop publishing and considers her involvement has helped her considerably in her search for a job: *'the centre gives me an opportunity to see vacancies on a more regular basis than if I had to travel to Worksop. While I have been coming here I have also had the chance to gain extra qualifications to help me in my job search'.*

G helps other clients to create a CV for job applications. She also helps clients to use computers. She recently became a member of the management committee and is looking forward to being more active in the centre's operations.

H became interested in the centre because of her interest in the community: *'It has helped me to become more confident and I have made some good friends'.* She has taken several computer courses and is now on the management committee. She has also joined the local Parish Council.

J first approached the centre when she needed information on welfare rights. She was then attracted to some of the courses offered in first aid, computing and desk-top publishing. She is currently taking courses in maths, English and food hygiene: *'I have gained a great deal of confidence through attending the Centre and have also made a lot of friends.'*

(Source: Visit to Langold Resource Centre and written information supplied)

The previous examples illustrate two patterns of informal learning: one where people have sought the help of a local agency to solve a specific problem, and one where learning has been incorporated within the activities of a local centre that is used for a variety of social and support purposes.

Informal learning is also frequently initiated by providers who approach existing groups in the community and negotiate learning programmes with them. A good example of this is Northern College in south Yorkshire. The college has a team of development officers who make contact with different community groups through non-educational networks and negotiate relevant learning activities such as short courses with them which are then delivered in community locations. These usually have a residential element and built-in progression options.

An incremental process

However it is generated, informal learning very frequently leads to continued learning although this may not have been initially planned or desired. Even when the learning is unpremeditated and unrecognised, there is often a point at which it becomes conscious and deliberate. Those involved in informal learning frequently develop new interests and identify additional information or skill needs which lead them into other learning activities. Many subsequently become confident and successful learners and are prepared to move to more formal programmes provided in other locations. Some studies have found that a significant proportion of entrants to programmes that are ostensible starting points – Return to Learn or access programmes – have previously engaged in informal learning in the community and it was this which gave them the confidence to seek a more structured learning pathway (McGivney, 1992).

The following examples illustrate how informal learning experiences can lead individuals into a learning pathway.

The Women's Education Project (now the **Women's Resource and Development Agency**) in Belfast was founded in the 1980s to provide educational opportunities for working-class women with no qualifications. To contact them, a project worker networked widely in the community and visited, at their request, groups of women who had come together in community locations and centres where crèches and playgroups had been established. In her discussions with the groups she was able to identify their most pressing concerns – health issues and lack of local services and amenities – and negotiate informal learning activities that might help to address these (discussion groups, contributions from guest speakers, etc). The initial activities acted as 'latch raisers' to a range of other topics – economic pressures, anxiety, depression, the stresses and strains of living in some areas of Belfast, and these formed the basis of subsequent learning courses that were jointly arranged with the groups. These in turn stimulated other learning interests and led to requests for courses in areas such as creative writing, organising and running community groups, fund-raising and informal tutoring.

As the women's confidence levels increased and their learning interests broadened, project workers provided information and advice on other local educational opportunities and referred women on where appropriate. They also organised a series of education information days involving all the main local providers.

In-depth evaluation of the project in 1989-1990 revealed that, as a result of their involvement, many previously unqualified women had become committed learners and had made extraordinary progress in their lives. Some had gone on to take qualifying courses at local colleges; some had become adult education tutors; some had found jobs and many had become active in their local communities. At the same time a number of women's groups had acquired the skills to self-organise, to fund-raise and to lobby politicians. Key factors favouring these outcomes were:

- Provision of negotiated, flexible, community-based learning activities, at no cost to learners.
- Provision of a crèche or financial support for childcare.

- Provision of advice and information on a range of issues including further learning opportunities.
- Brokering and referrals (putting groups in contact with other information and education agencies).
- Provision of practical help and support (with fund-raising proposals, educational materials, etc). (McGivney, 1990)

In the 1980s, a Birmingham local authority community development officer initiated informal learning activities for women on **Castle Vale Estate**. The approach was to provide childcare for pre-school children and social and recreational activities for mothers at the local community centre. Open coffee mornings allowed the women to get together and engage in activities such as Keep Fit while their children were safely looked after in a play-scheme. Their shared interest in young children led to the setting up of an informal discussion group using Open University materials on child development. For a number of the women, participation in this stimulated an interest in further learning and some courses were then set up for them by the local education authority and the then Pre-School Playgroups Association. A large number of women subsequently moved on from these to more formal, certificated education and training courses as well as into paid or voluntary employment. Their diverse progression routes illustrate the characteristic 'zig-zag' pattern of adult learning trajectories mentioned on page 9. (See McGivney, 1992, Figure 2, p 23.)

The features favouring these outcomes were:
- Provision of non-threatening informal activities in a familiar local venue.
- Gradual introduction of a range of other educational opportunities,

and, crucially,
- The encouragement and enthusiasm of a of a community development worker with a knowledge and understanding of other local education opportunities. (McGivney, 1992)

In both of these examples, the key factors that brought women back into learning were: 1) the opportunity to meet in a familiar local venue at which childcare was offered, and, 2) the intervention of a 'key' person who negotiated and arranged learning activities in response to expressed interests and concerns.

The following examples are of informal learning activities that were initiated by outside agencies in response to the needs they perceived as arising out of the circumstances of particular groups. In both cases the activities offered, as well as being beneficial in themselves, helped many individuals to take new directions in their lives:

Lightbowne Young Families Project is a community and family project in the Moston area of north Manchester which was established to enhance the physical, social, emotional and welfare needs of young families in the area. The project is part of the Salford Family Service Unit and is funded through the North Manchester Single Regeneration Budget. The steering group includes representative from Children's Services, Social Services, the Health Authority, the Local Residents' Association and the Family Service Unit.

The project focuses specifically on the development of parenting and childcare skills, the improvement of levels of 'risk', and local priorities such as health issues and diet. Between

1995 and 1998 it worked with 79 women, the majority of them single parents, and over 100 children.

The project provides an adult and toddler drop-in session; a homework club for children from the local primary school and an educational group programme for adults supported by a crèche. The group programme began when the project moved to its own premises in September 1996. Between 1996 and 1998, there were 32 groups, covering a wide range of subject areas including health, diet, drama, children's play and education, personal and social development, relaxation, vocational interests and family support. Each group is led by a member of staff, outside facilitators and, more recently, by learners who have progressed to take on a facilitator's role.

Participants in the programme have identified a number of benefits both to themselves and their children: significantly raised confidence and self-esteem, greater understanding of play and child development, ability to develop play, to make educational things, better family relationships.

The longer-term gains have been progression to activities previously considered impossible or out of reach. Some parents have become involved in their children's school for the first time as readers, classroom volunteers and helpers on outside trips. Others have started to co-lead groups in the project or have taken up employment. Some women have enrolled on formal courses such as NVQs in child care and office skills:

'The Lightbowne Project has acted as both a bridge and a support into these other activities' (…) Parents and children learn simultaneously – upstairs and downstairs. The learning in both groups reinforces the other. Whilst the children are playing to learn, the parents are learning to use play as a developmental activity for their children and themselves: "it's a chance to learn more – furthering both mine and my child's education". The parents are stimulated and encouraged, and go on to develop this stimulation with the children away from the project (…). One Lightbowne project user, when interviewed, confirmed that the project was for her: "a step from nowhere to somewhere, a step from home to college, a means of achieving my career goal and not sitting on the social for the rest of my life".' (Chew and Platten, 1998: 18)

Since 1991 a course entitled **Under Fives Play and Disability** has been running at the **Play Centre**, at Sherwood in Nottingham, funded by Greater Nottingham TEC and WEA. The course was the idea of development workers attached to the project who felt that there was a need for raising awareness of the needs of children with disabilities and their families. They approached the WEA who developed a short, informal non-accredited course which was run successfully at a local and accessible community centre before being moved to purpose-built premises.

The programme, which is now accredited through the North East Midlands Access Partnership (NEMAP), helps participants – parents, voluntary workers and professionals – to explore the range and extent of disabilities affecting children and to consider the ways in which these can be incorporated into a wide range of play activities. Delivery includes learning through play, group activities, case studies, project work and guest speakers. Interactive learning methods have been designed to raise awareness of issues such as integration, equal opportunities, organising play and obtaining resources.

Most participants produce a portfolio of resources by the end of the course including play materials that they have created.

Participants' progression routes have been very varied. Individuals have moved on to a variety of other education and training courses including an Open University degree course and training trainer courses. Some have become involved in other child-related projects such as toy libraries and parents' support groups. Others have taken on voluntary activities in the community and some have gained employment. Examples of new jobs include Social Services trainer in Epilepsy, Disability Officer in the Inland Revenue and play leader in a local group. (Source: Cheryl Turner, NIACE, and documentation produced by project workers)

These varied examples of community-based learning confirm that people frequently embark on a learning pathway as a result of:

- Facilities or activities provided in a familiar, non-threatening local environment.
- The interventions and encouragement of specific agencies or individuals.
- The opportunity to have a say in the nature and implementation of the activities undertaken.
- The relevance of initial learning activities to learner circumstances, interests and concerns.
- The removal of any practical, situational and psychological barriers that may have prevented them from engaging in learning in the past.

Local venues

The first of these – the siting of learning in a familiar local environment – is the major factor in widening participation. This was repeatedly stressed during the visits and contacts made during this study:

> *The overriding factor [in widening participation] is geography: how near or far you are from a centre of learning.* (outreach worker)
> *You won't get people from here going to the city centre: they need re-establishment in the community first.* (guidance worker)

Research into the benefits of pre-schools for parents (McGivney, 1998) revealed that *none* of respondents who had participated in courses provided by the Pre-School Learning Alliance had been seeking the same type of course elsewhere. Without exception, all had participated because courses were drawn to their attention through the group and were delivered in the familiar local environment.

The success of the BBC Education *Computers Don't Bite* initiative can be attributed in part to the siting of some of the taster sessions in informal local venues such as libraries, schools, football clubs, pubs, supermarkets, cafés and community centres, as well as to the enormous interest in learning to use computers within the population.

Relevance

Relevance to local interests and concerns is another significant factor in widening participation as well as in subsequent progression. A Community Education and Local Enterprise project conducted between 1992 and 1994 by the community education service in Coventry tested a number of learning models for disadvantaged, long-term unemployed people. The model that produced the greatest number of people achieving qualifications, entering further education or entering paid or unpaid or voluntary work was the one which had developed programmes around the needs of people involved in community activities such as running tenants' and community groups. (City of Coventry Community Education Service, undated).

Rates of educational progression

How many people who return to learning informally in the community subsequently make the transition to formal education or training? The question is frequently asked but is difficult to answer except in relation to specific learning situations. Although it is generally accepted that informal learning can be the starting point of a pathway leading to formal learning, quantitative evidence on a national scale is impossible to find for a number of reasons:

- Informal learning is very diverse and takes place in a huge number and variety of settings.
- Much of it is small in scale with a local focus and precarious funding.
- Community-based learning is often spontaneous and embedded in the routine activities of an organisation, therefore progression outcomes are not analysed.
- To track learners who move horizontally and vertically through different sectors and institutions as their needs and circumstances change would require collaboration and harmonisation of student tracking methodologies. However, there are wide differences between sectors, organisations and institutions in their record-keeping and student follow-up procedures.
- Many community-based groups and organisations do not have the resources to keep track of former users. Moreover they may not be required to do so.
- Informal learning is often perceived to be of low status and therefore of little interest to educational professionals. Those who have been involved in informal and uncertificated learning do not always mention it when moving into formal education programmes.

Studies that have sought evidence of rates of progression between different kinds and levels of learning have come up against many or all of these problems. A previous NIACE study, *Tracking Adult Learning Routes* (McGivney, 1992), found little quantitative evidence on the extent of movement between different forms and levels of learning. This was partly due to the difficulties involved in tracking learners across different sectors and institutions with different information systems. At the time of the study, few adult education centres or further and higher education institutions had student tracking strategies and this was exacerbated by a lack of articulation and linkages between formal and less formal education programmes. Information from a range of individual sources nevertheless suggested that a number of individuals from groups under-represented in formal education and training had returned to learning informally in community education, local projects and voluntary organisations, and were subsequently motivated to engage in more formal programmes.

Another NIACE study (McGivney, 1994) investigated the extent of progression between different forms and levels of learning in the Taff Ely area of south Wales. The findings reflected those of other studies in showing that participation in learning of any kind could stimulate a desire to continue learning. However, as elsewhere, this process was not systematically monitored and was therefore difficult to quantify. At the time of the study few providers had systems in place for tracking students although the situation was changing in response to new further and higher education funding requirements. The study nevertheless provided evidence of educational progression at three stages:

- *from non-participation to participation*. Informal learning in community settings was providing a route back into learning for many women and people with few qualifications as well as for some adults who already had formal qualifications but wanted to regain a learning habit. As a result of prior learning experiences in the community (sometimes in non-educational environments), a number of individuals had developed a taste for learning and wished to pursue more structured and higher levels of learning.

- *from one subject to another at the same level*. Many respondents participating in community education had already attended a range of courses in the same venue and a number expressed an interest in taking courses in other subjects.

- *from one educational level to a higher level in the same subject in the same or another institution*. There was a flow, or perhaps more accurately, a steady trickle, of people moving from informal courses to more advanced level work, especially where the subjects learned had a logical next learning step (e.g. from an introductory course to a higher level course). The local technical college was the best known and most attractive next destination for adults involved in informal learning.

Like the previous NIACE project (McGivney, 1992), this one suggested that educational progression was hampered by lack of links between sectors and insufficient articulation between community-based and institutional-based education and between informal, non-accredited and more formal, accredited programmes.

A similar finding emerged from a study conducted in Scotland:

> To date there have been few developments which ensure the articulation of all community-based adult learning opportunities with more formal provision. Opportunities for progression are not always clearly defined for community-based learners. (Scottish Office, 1996: 8-9)

Several years on, there are signs of a growing recognition of the need to provide learners with progression options, and in some areas there have been comprehensive attempts to articulate general, non-accredited provision (non-Schedule 2) with Further Education Funding Council programmes. The London Borough of Harrow, for example, supports adult education programmes through a contract with the three tertiary colleges in the borough and closely monitors the outcomes. In 1996 a survey was conducted in the borough to assess whether appropriate progression options were in place for learners on the LEA-sponsored programme; how freely they could move from non-Schedule 2 to FEFC courses, and the level of interest in certification and accreditation within non-Schedule 2 programmes. The survey found that although patterns of movement from LEA-sponsored to FEFC courses were fluid and complex, some specific patterns could be identified:

- Where LEA courses were designed as stepping-stones (eg. IT and communications) virtually all LEA students moved on to a qualification course.

- Where LEA courses were free-standing but had a clear qualification follow-up option (for example, a ten-week counselling course at one college leading directly to certificate and diploma courses at another), a significant minority of students progressed immediately to the FEFC option. (This was seen as a very effective model that might be expanded by provision of lead-in or taster sessions.)

- In some subject areas such as modern languages, learners were moving backwards and forwards between qualification and non-Schedule 2 courses to develop the required level of skills. These included learners who had completed qualification courses and were looking for skills updating.

- In some areas such as crafts (dressmaking/fashion, cake decoration and soft furnishings) learners wanted progression options but had chosen to continue in LEA provision rather than moving to a qualification course for reasons such as reluctance to learn in a different college or local area.

• No movement from LEA to qualification courses.

Overall, it was estimated that about a fifth of students who enrolled in LEA provision later joined FEFC-funded courses. In many cases participation in non-Schedule 2 provision had played a significant part in their decision to move into qualification courses. Progression rates may also have been helped by the fact that both part-time non-Schedule 2 and qualification courses were offered in the same institutions and were advertised side by side, implying parity of value and status (Adkins, 1997).

As the Harrow survey suggests, movement between different levels of learning is significantly helped by the existence of clear learning routes. The importance of these and other factors in facilitating educational progression will be discussed in the following section.

3 Strategies and factors that assist learner progression

There are a number of well established adult learning pathways. In an address to a NIACE conference (*Learning Pathways*, 1 December 1998), David Melville, Chief Executive of the FEFC, described these as *'so diverse that we should not speak of a pathway but of 'an integrated motorway and rail system.'*

Australian research (McIntyre and Kimberley, 1998) has identified a number of pathway models all of which have equivalents in this country. These include:

- *Entry or starting point models* (Learning pathways from informal non-accredited courses which provide a positive experience of learning in a supportive environment and which may be linked to follow-on options).
- *Adult literacy*: (often a key starting point which can be linked to or incorporated in other learning programmes).
- *Employment path models*: (Pathways from informal community-based programmes which allow people to create, prepare for, or take advantage of local employment opportunities).
- *Integrated models* (A range of options provided by one provider with visible links between them, for example from a basic education starting point to accredited courses).
- *Provider partnership models* (Pathways to education and training created by inter-agency co-operation).
- *Community development models* (Progression routes enabled by community-based services such as community centres, groups and organisations which provide a comprehensive social, educational and employment programme and bring a range of services together).
- *Unpaid worker or volunteer routes* (Pathways to formal education, training and employment from unpaid voluntary work in the community).
- *Culturally appropriate pathways* (Learning routes developed for specific social or ethnic groups which respond to their diverse education, employment and support needs).
- *State-wide progression strategies* (National or regional strategies that facilitate transition between different learning environments and levels of learning eg. credit transfer arrangements; APEL).
- *Open learning and ICT strategies* (Pathways for homebound or isolated communities and individuals provided by open and ICT-based learning in a range of locations).

If one were to adapt this typology to the UK there are other models one might add, such as the Access route model. From the point of view of informal learning, however, a significant conclusion of the Australian study (which focused specifically on women's learning routes) was that the flexible and responsive community development model was the best developed approach to planning learning pathways from informal learning:

Pathway planning is facilitated where it is an integral part of community-based practice. Pathways are most readily arranged by providers who are responding to the needs of their communities by providing a range of options, and where they understand pathways development from adult community education in a holistic way. (. . .) A pathway is not limited to setting up an arrangement to link one course to another. It is much more about setting up options for learners and assisting them to take the directions which they feel ready to take on the strength of their learning. (McIntyre and Kimberley, 1998: 54)

This study confirmed the validity of these assertions and provided insights into some of the factors and conditions that lead people from informal into formal learning.

Factors favouring progression

Previous research into the factors that facilitate learner progression (McGivney, 1992 and 1995) concluded that progression from informal and uncertificated learning to more advanced levels of education and training often depends less on the subject or level of the prior learning than on a range of specific factors and preconditions. In both studies, information from a range of statutory and voluntary providers indicated that adults most often move from informal learning into more formal and certificated programmes when there are particular arrangements and mechanisms in place that help and encourage them to do so. Notable among these were:

- Staff encouragement, support and knowledge of other learning opportunities.
- Collaboration and partnerships between sectors, institutions and organisations to create a range of opportunities.
- Information and guidance services with good referral procedures within and between providing organisations and institutions.
- Clear and well developed progression routes with linkages between non-credit courses and formal accredited courses.
- Articulation between outreach provision and mainstream programmes.
- Systems such as credit frameworks, Open College Networks, Access consortia, Credit Accumulation and Transfer schemes.
- Systems to accredit prior learning and experience acquired outside a formal learning environment (APEL).
- Modularised or unit-based courses allowing for recognition of small achievements.
- Support mechanisms to help overcome adults' barriers to learning (help with costs, travel and childcare; flexible and appropriate course timing and delivery).
- Learning support in areas such as Study Skills, Literacy, Numeracy, English, Welsh.

The importance of such factors in encouraging people to continue learning and to move to successively more demanding programmes of study have been confirmed in other studies (for example, Munn, Tett and Arney, 1993; Maxwell, 1997).

As the list suggests, progression routes are created and enabled by *structures and infrastructures* (responsive providers and systems; collaborative arrangements and networking; guidance services); by *curriculum and accreditation strategies* (provision designed to assist progression (access courses, etc); modular approaches; accreditation frameworks; APEL), and by learning and learner *support mechanisms*. This study demonstrated that, in the case of informal learning, there is an even more important factor involved in widening participation and encouraging educational progression: *people*.

Key people

The information collected for this study suggests that one of the most important prerequisites in encouraging individuals to embark and continue on a learning pathway is the intervention of 'key' individuals who inform, advise, encourage and enthuse informal learners and motivate and help them to engage in new activities. Sometimes these are specialist guidance workers or education outreach workers trained in the delivery of guidance, but very often they are not. Many of the people who are instrumental in spreading information and encouraging people to engage and continue in learning are from non-educational organisations and networks. In some areas, for example, health visitors and crèche or playgroup workers play an important part in disseminating information and linking people with education providers. NIACE research in Northern Ireland (McGivney, 1990) found that women who had become involved in learning had often been provided with information, advice, contacts and practical help by neighbourhood and community workers as well as by community education workers. These had helped women's groups to become established and had contributed to the expansion of their activities by supplying information on sources of help and expertise and referring them to educational agencies that the women would have not previously have known about or considered approaching.

It is well established that the most effective recruitment method in adult education is word of mouth. As one informant put it: *'The big pulling point is the grapevine'*.

People who are well known and trusted in a community, irrespective of their occupation, often play a crucial role in spreading information and encouraging people to undertake learning activities. A college outreach worker developing learning opportunities in the east of England has found that the most useful contacts are:

> *those who already had a presence and credibility in the community, something which can take years to develop. It undoubtedly helps that, like many of my clients, I have lived locally for many years (...) People recognise me from school and the locality and realise that I share many of their concerns.* (Blackwell, 1997)

In a junior school visited during the course of this study, a parent volunteer is a key conduit of information about literacy workshops and other school-based adult learning opportunities. She is able to convince other parents that these are acceptable and worthwhile activities and manages to infect them with her own enthusiasm. In workplaces, the key person may be a manager, a fellow worker, a shop steward, mentor or union representative. One informant reported that in his organisation the office cleaner is the most important disseminator of information about learning opportunities.

Sometimes the 'key' people comprise a proactive group who have come together specifically to provide informal learning for others in their community.

CHAWS (Community Health Activists Workington South) is a group of women who had attended Community Health Matters courses designed to train community health activities at grassroots level, provided by the WEA and North Cumbria Health Development Unit. The group was set up in 1997 to raise awareness of health issues among local residents, to provide education and training on health issues and to initiate and participate in health campaigns. The group meets every week for planning purposes and their activities to date include the production of community health newsletters; membership of the North Cumbria Health

Action Zone and the Community Health Activists' Steering Group; collaboration with the Health Authority on a home safety campaign and organisation of a conference for community health activists in Cumbria. They have also developed a website for community health activists and negotiated with local providers to provide relevant short courses. In their work with local people, CHAWS recognises that many are not confident enough to join courses so the approach is to make contact with people through informal activities such as children's parties and line dancing. (Brown, 1999)

Animateurs and role models

People working in the former coalfield areas have found that local people who have wide networks and are trusted in the community have insights into local problems and needs that can inform the style and content of learning provision. When such people themselves engage successfully in employment, learning or community activities, they become positive role models and encourage others to believe that they could do likewise. When they take on tutor or facilitator roles: *'this positive influence is greatly intensified'* (CLIP, 1998).

There is growing recognition of the need to develop the skills of local people so that they can raise the educational awareness of other members of their communities and point them towards opportunities. This kind of capacity-building is particularly important in areas where there are few facilities and where, to quote a community education worker, *'if people get on they usually get out'*.

A number of education institutions and community organisations contacted during the study had initiated schemes to train local people to act as community facilitators, learning champions or 'signposters' to education and training: *'These workers – animateurs, social entrepreneurs, agents of change – are crucial to the process [of widening participation]'.* (CLIP, 1998)

Examples of initiatives to develop the skills of local people to help their communities are given below:

Park Lane College is developing a negotiated accredited training programme – **Community Volunteer Training** – for people involved in voluntary organisations in Leeds. The idea is to develop a cascade model, helping people from local communities to develop their communication skills so that they can facilitate informal learning activities with small groups. This will enable the college to embed some of the informal, non-accredited programmes it currently runs in the community on short-term funding.
(Source: Park Lane College)

Fast Forward, a county-wide education strategy in Nottinghamshire, has successfully piloted **Signposter** training projects. These provide NVQ-accredited training, work placements and job search support for small teams of volunteers who will provide a specialist local service providing information and guidance on education, training and employment. Trainees develop a range of highly transferable skills through their training and, at the same time, provide an accessible information service in their own communities.

One of the projects was run in Newark. It involved a range of partners from both the statutory and voluntary sectors. It started in April 1998 and recruited a small team of 10 local residents. They had an initial two-day induction programme before starting the programme under the guidance of a supervisor from Guideline Careers Services. At the same time as doing their NVQ training, members of the group were providing guidance in their own communities. It is intended to extend the project to other areas and to groups who already provide information without the benefit of training.

Another programme being developed with Fast Forward support is the **Mansfield Animateur Project** (MAP). This aims to train local unemployed or unwaged people as community organisers or animateurs. The idea is to provide accredited training with work placements focusing on local economic development, national decision-making and funding processes. Trainees will be expected to pass on their new skills and understanding to their communities and contribute towards local regeneration. At the same time they can enhance their own employment prospects. (Source: Fast Forward)

The Voluntary Sector Training Group in Northamptonshire is working to increase access to training for people working in the sector as staff or volunteers. It provides short training courses and a regular handbook, distributed via the CVS mailing list, highlighting the courses available from social services and voluntary organisations that will share their training. The group acts as a link and broker between sectors and providers and raises awareness of the opportunities available. (Source: Helen Butler, Northants Voluntary Sector Training Group).

In Somerset, the Community Education Service is developing the concept of **Community Learning Champions**. DfEE funding for Adult and Community projects has been used to fund the project which is providing training for 10 individuals from local community groups and organisations. The programme is based on the accredited Volunteer, Support and Training programme and trains participants to offer information to local people on learning opportunities. Participants are provided with an information base on local learning pathways and a system of ongoing support. (Source: Somerset Community Education Service).

Communities in Crisis project in Greater Manchester provides adults who are active in their communities with training, support and resources to help them resolve local problems and issues that they themselves have identified.

The project involves a group of up to 24 people. It has a structured programme of training days (including a short residential period) the content and input of which is negotiated with participants. Individuals from a number of groups (eg. women's health groups, tenants' groups, self-help groups) are contacted and encouraged to join the project for 12 months, during which time they produce a report reflecting their progress and achievements. Participants tend to be low paid or unemployed, with poor early schooling and little experience of post 16 education. (Batten *et al*, 1993)

Sharing Credit is a project of the National Voluntary and Community Sector Accreditation Consortium based at the University of Derby. There are five members – the National Association of Councils for Voluntary Service (NACVS), the National Association of Volunteer Bureaux, the British Association of Settlement and Social Action Centres,

Federation of Community Work Training Groups and the National Open College Network.

The project has been using Lottery money to develop strategies at a regional level to accredit learning and training for its members and users; to encourage and develop the ability of the sector to accredit activity, and to encourage a culture of learning within the sector. It is also mapping good practice by identifying progression routes from non-accredited learning to higher levels among workers and users in the voluntary sector. The project has a particular focus on encouraging networks to use National Open College Network and other credit frameworks and is working regionally and locally with development agencies to take account of local needs. The intention is to develop regional sub-groups and hold meetings to highlight and disseminate good practice. The project has already piloted a 'tool kit' to help groups see their way through the jungle of qualifications and accreditation processes

Sharing Credit is also involved in the Unit Bank – a bank of learning and training units which helps groups or individuals to access nationally recognised units in areas such as volunteer training, working in voluntary organisations, working with older people, youth work in rural areas, running community buildings, managing voluntary organisations and equal opportunities training. It also helps organisations working in partnership to obtain funding for accredited training and learning. (Source: *Sharing Credit*)

Development work in the community

The education providers which are most effective in widening participation and helping people to move from informal into formal learning are those which have invested in community outreach or development workers.

One of the main skills required of those working in the community, especially when targeting particularly disadvantaged groups, is the ability to gain the cooperation and trust of the *'gatekeepers'*: the people who are most in contact with specific communities such as probation officers, playgroup leaders, wardens of residential homes and day centres, etc.: *'We need to make contact not just with individuals and groups; we also need to sensitise those working with them'* (community outreach worker). The study indicated that this dimension of work in the community is critical in widening participation and helping individuals and groups onto a learning pathway.

In their work with groups suffering from multiple deprivation, outreach staff from **Park Lane College Leeds** meet first with probation officers, agencies working with the homeless, residents' associations, and others, and discuss the kinds of learning activities that might assist the respective groups. They find that they often have to challenge the gatekeepers' 'over-protectiveness' towards the groups they are working with or who are in their charge: *'They often say "they won't be able to do this or that". We raise their aspirations for the groups they're working with and make them aware of possibilities.'*

A careful and diplomatic approach to the gatekeepers enables the development workers to tailor informal learning programmes to the requirements of target groups. For example, using European funding, they have worked in hostels for homeless people, offering courses in DIY, life skills and first aid (for problems such as drug overdosing, stab wounds).

The work is informal, responsive to needs, unaccredited and, inevitably, short term. However, workers always try and point individuals in other directions:

'Some disappear but others come into college or go onto the Prince's Trust. Some young homeless

people started with us on informal learning, then went on to accredited work. Some then joined Raleigh International and are now working abroad.' (Source: Park Lane College)

Chesterton Community College in Cambridge has an outreach worker who contacts agencies and groups in the community and provides information, guidance and learning opportunities for groups such as the unemployed, minority ethnic communities, people without qualifications, people in low income groups and lone parents. A special budget enables her to reduce some of the barriers to participation, for example by offering free places and help with childcare.

To reach groups, the worker networks with a wide range of professionals and agencies – probation officers, head teachers, church leaders, health visitors, community development workers, youth workers, social workers, women's and other voluntary groups, councillors, tenants' associations, careers guidance workers, the Benefits Agency, the Job Centre and other further education providers. Through building these links she has been able to identify a variety of community learning needs and respond by setting up informal learning activities in local venues. She has also arranged monthly drop-in sessions at a local community house. This provides a safe and informal space for people to meet and explore options. One outcome has been the organisation of fortnightly craft sessions. For less confident learners these have proved to be a stepping stone to more demanding courses.

The outreach approach is responsive, flexible and supportive:

'We are prepared to run these sorts of courses for smaller than average numbers at very low cost, and will always consider an open-ended approach if that is what the participants need. Through listening, advising, encouraging, guiding and supporting (literally holding hands in some instances) and always following up to check progress, it has been possible to enable people to participate. For many, meeting the tutor beforehand or attending a small class in a local community centre has been a thoroughly enjoyable experience and has fostered the belief that education, in its broadest sense, is for them. The knock-on effect can be very rewarding, such as a client informing you that she has got a full-time job as a result of the confidence she gained from participating on a course, or chatting with some children who proudly announce that their mum's 'gone back to school' to learn about computers'.

The worker keeps records of the people she has worked with. These show that of 108 individuals contacted during the initial months of her appointment, 17 had enrolled on Schedule 2 and 12 on non-Schedule 2 courses. Nineteen others had become active in different ways, attending the monthly drop-ins, getting more involved in their children's schooling or attending the craft sessions. (Blackwell, 1997)

An outreach guidance worker based at **Royal Forest of Dean College** networks with a range of rural groups and agencies including Family Centres (social and support centres set up for pre-school children and their families) and Opportunity Centres (for disabled children, those with learning difficulties and their families). The worker visits the centres on a regular basis and talks informally to leaders and users. On the basis of the needs and interests identified, she then sets up short, informal, ESF-funded courses for parents.

She has also worked with Gloucester Mental Health Association, Women's Refuge, a centre for the unemployed and an information shop for young people (Cinderford Area

Neighbourhood Initiative) where she gives advice to groups and individuals and organises parenting classes for young single parents.

The information, guidance and informal learning activities she provides often encourage individuals to enrol in college courses. When this happens, the guidance worker continues to help individuals by providing information, support and help with things like travel and childcare. She also helps people with what may seem like minor details but ones which can be critical to a successful transition to formal education: telling them: *'which door to use; where the car park is, and so on'*. (Source: visit to college and information from guidance staff)

Without this kind of development work in the community there would be little possibility of widening participation in education among the most excluded and deprived groups.

4 Responsive providers and systems

Successful transitions from informal to formal learning also depend on the existence of appropriate learning routes. In many areas, the WEA, local authorities and community education providers, colleges with good outreach systems, residential colleges and voluntary organisations are developing practical and imaginative responses to continuing learning interests in the community.

Community-based outreach provision

For people who are unable or not sufficiently confident to approach a formal institution, outreach programmes provide important progression opportunities.

> *Although the standard of delivery should never be compromised, it may, in certain circumstances, be advantageous to settle for an adequate level of resourcing in the community rather than high resource levels and delivery within an institution.* (Scottish Office, 1996: 27)

Well developed outreach work can significantly assist in widening participation and encouraging progression between informal and formal learning, as the following examples demonstrate.

Gloucester Adult and Continuing Education and Training offers non-accredited community education provision in a wide range of community venues in rural areas – leisure centres, village or parish halls, youth and community centres, enterprise centres. Although students are not systematically tracked, it is generally found that these act as tasters and a number of people move on to other courses.

Park Lane College in Leeds provides learning opportunities at a large number of sites dispersed around the city, using non-Schedule 2, European and FEFC funding. The community-based work involves contact and networking with a large number of other organisations and services, including schools, Family Service Units, the Education Support Agency, the Probation Service, the Youth Service, NHS trusts, voluntary organisations, Leeds Play Network, the local TEC, Mental Health Advocacy and health groups: *'These organisations and groups often run informal support groups. They often make contact with us'*.

Short learning activities are mounted in response to identified interests and concerns and it is often found that these stimulate an interest in more structured, formal learning:
'We use non-Schedule 2 or ESF funding to run first step or day sessions on a particular issue of

interest or concern expressed by the group. From these short courses people gain interest to do things in more depth and this leads to tailor-made courses. Learning packages are put together to enable people to progress to higher levels, either for a group or on an individual basis'.

The college outreach provision is staged in a way that enables new learners to progress gradually from locally-based learning to main college sites. The step-by-step approach is considered very important:

'Progression is very local. They start in informal groups and that's the kick start; then they can move to a bigger setting but it's still local e.g. a college outreach site. And finally they may go to college where there is a broader range of educational offerings. Many wouldn't have come through this door if we hadn't gone first into their own territory.'
(Source: Park Lane College)

Although Park Lane College provision is very widely dispersed, it is locked into the college framework of provision and quality procedures. This is very important. All studies of progression show that, however informal they are, outreach courses and other learning activities should not be isolated, one-off events. It is essential to learning pathways that they are articulated with mainstream provision and subjected to the same quality assurance procedures that are applied in the host institution.

This study also indicated that responses to learning needs identified during outreach work have to be prompt in order to maintain learner momentum and enthusiasm:

*If learning interests are identified you've got to do it **now**. There's no point is saying something will be starting in September.* (Community education worker)

You have to have programmes running at all times so that people can start at any time. When they trickle in, you need to give them something that day, not next September.
(College outreach worker)

Regional or county-wide initiatives

In some areas there have been county-wide efforts to widen participation and encourage the least socially and educationally advantaged groups to embark on a learning pathway.

Fast Forward helps people living in Nottinghamshire to return to education, training and employment and participate in local decision-making and community regeneration.
The principal aims are:

- to encourage and support the first steps back into education and training for adults who would not normally participate.
- to work creatively to identify the needs of local communities, to act as a catalyst to fill gaps in existing provision and to influence mainstream activity by developing more appropriate and sustainable provision.

The scheme is funded by the County Council from a variety of sources including the Single Regeneration Budget, the Rural Development Commission and Europe. It runs in community settings throughout the county and works with a wide range of partners to develop locally-based learning opportunities and progression routes into further training or employment. It also provides help with the costs of childcare, travel and other things when these act as a barrier to access or progression.

In the north of the county, the scheme operates through 'Lead Agent' colleges. These administer individual support on behalf of *Fast Forward* and deliver most of the provision themselves although they may use other providers to meet some identified interests and needs. In 1996-1997, *Fast Forward* together with Nottinghamshire County Council, North Nottinghamshire College and the North Nottinghamshire Training and Enterprise Council supported new opportunities for over 800 Bassetlaw residents. In Langold, the scheme supported delivery of a range of programmes for local residents including Computing (CLAIT), British Red Cross Basic First Aid, an Introduction to Sign Language and the ASDAN Further Education Awards for volunteers in the community. At the Women's Resource Centre in Worksop, *Fast Forward* offered computer workshops, English and Maths and Basic First Aid. It also supported International Women's Day with child care, information technology and advice and guidance.

In the Greater Nottingham area the scheme works through 'Compact Operations Groups' (COGs) which bring providers together in partnership. In these areas, the *Fast Forward* Partnership worker identifies local learning needs and responds in the most appropriate way, where necessary with another agency or provider.

The local learning activities provided under the scheme are funded by the LEA, ESF and FEFC. This enables *Fast Forward* to support both non-accredited and accredited learning programmes in a wide range of community venues without losing the informal nature of the learning. There are also links between the *Fast Forward* programme and non-Schedule 2 activities funded by the County Council Adult Education budget, much of which are delivered in primary schools.

Since 1997-98 advice and guidance have been incorporated into all supported activities in community settings. This helps to make people aware of progression possibilities. *Fast Forward* also encourages progression by offering county residents who are unemployed, receiving benefits or on low incomes financial support for entering an accredited programme of education or training in a college. On enrolling, eligible individuals are required to attend an initial guidance interview after which they sign an agreement with the college and draw up an individual progression plan.

In 1997, *Fast Forward* helped 3,307 people to return to education and training. Features of the scheme that favour widening participation and progression are:

- Collaboration and partnership with a wide range of agencies
- Use of different funding sources for provision
- Flexibility and responsiveness to expressed interests and needs
- Support for provision of taster and basic courses that motivate people to progress onto accredited programmes of study
- Use of local settings for delivery of informal provision
- Support with costs and childcare
- Practical support for residents on low incomes to enter accredited college programmes.

(Source: *Fast Forward*)

Drome is an education and training partnership organised in Flintshire by the Welsh College of Horticulture and Deeside College in association with the University of Wales, Bangor. The partnership involves collaboration between further and higher education, adult residential providers and a network of statutory and voluntary organisations working at a community level across North Wales. The aims are:

- To provide opportunities for adults to return to learning and have a positive educational experience.
- To enable adults to explore their personal potential, grow in confidence and self-esteem and develop awareness of the range of potential progression opportunities available to them.
- To enable adults to recognise the value of their own achievements.
- To provide access to a range of progression opportunities.

The programme operates on a borough district basis, with tutor-organisers responsible for the development, management and organisation of the programme, local networking and student support. Within each district, a programme comprising Foundation and Further Opportunity modules is offered. *The Foundation Programme* is based on a Second Chance to Learn model with emphasis on personal development and building confidence, self-esteem, and cultural awareness. The *Further Opportunity* programme has a range of introductory modules with a pre-vocational emphasis spanning the creative arts, business, social sciences, horticulture, engineering, information technology, and environmental science, all of which can lead to higher levels of further education or training. Students are guided in choosing modules and progression routes to other opportunities.

About 1,200 people participate in *Drome* each academic year. A survey conducted of those who had participated in one or more module during 1993-94 showed that participation had led to significant personal development gains, with over 80 per cent of all (950) respondents considering that participation had improved their self-confidence, their ability to express ideas and opinions, their ability to take part in group activities, see different points of view, and develop new friendships. A significant number also felt they had acquired useful skills and knowledge, gained new interests and broadened their interests. In addition:

- 50 per cent had progressed to employment
- 14 per cent had moved into other areas of education and training
- 16 per cent had taken on voluntary work
- 21 per cent had joined a local hobby or interest group

The survey showed that individual learners were likely to follow more than one progression route. For example:

- 14 per cent had undertaken further learning activities and joined a local group
- 10 per cent had undertaken further learning activities and progressed to paid work
- 8 per cent had undertaken further learning activities and progressed to voluntary work.

A significant finding was that learners were more likely to progress to education and training when there was a liberal element to their programme. Those who had participated in both the Foundation and the Further Opportunity programme were significantly more likely than other students to progress to Schedule 2a courses, while those who had participated in the Foundation Programme were significantly more likely than other students to enrol in GCSEs and A Levels as well as in uncertificated learning. Those who had taken the Foundation

Programme were also more likely than average to move along all the identified progression routes: 'The *findings highlight the importance of programmes encompassing both liberal and vocational studies in facilitating progression'*.

A number of features of *Drome* were identified as promoting progression. These include:

- Enjoyable return-to-learn experiences encouraging growth of self-confidence.
- Help to develop awareness of capabilities, self-direction and learner autonomy.
- Friendly and encouraging tutors.
- Group learning.
- Courses relevant to work opportunities and working routines.
- Provision of information and guidance.
- A step-by step approach to learning and guidance.
- A modular programme structure accredited by the OCN.
- Preparation for progression: (help in learning "how to learn"; introduction to teaching and assessment methods used at the next stages of education and training).
- Visible and well defined progression routes into most areas of education and training facilitated by collaboration between providers and networks
- Speakers and visits linked to progression opportunities.
- Open College Network procedures that assist progression to education and training.

(Source: Maxwell, 1997)

Partnerships

A key feature of the last two examples is their collaborative nature. The development of progression frameworks enabling people to move between different learning environments, subjects and learning levels requires the prior establishment of effective relationships and working partnerships between all relevant providers and agencies:

> *Without effective cross-sectoral networking providers cannot devise articulated programmes in community locations. In some areas of the country, providers are unclear of the roles and potential of other agencies. This can result in overlap or, in some instances, a failure to identify gaps in provision. Adult learning networks offer excellent opportunities to clarify roles, share expertise and resources and plan joint learning and training programmes.* (Scottish Office, 1996: 30)

Partnership and networking between organisations, groups and institutions involve both formal and informal links. Sometimes these are generated at manager level and sometimes at lower staff levels. Personal relationships have been found considered particularly important in the development of learning routes:

> *The personal contact between members of different institutions was seen as equally important as more formal meetings between different bodies. This was true right across the spectrum of provision. One college access co-ordinator spoke of the importance of being able to speak directly to a contact in a receiving institution when developing individual learning programmes. Similarly, a community school tutor emphasised the need to be able to obtain direct and swift answers from a college contact when dealing with adult enquiries.* (Munn, Tett and Arney, 1993: 28)

However, arrangements that are over-dependent on personal relationships may be fragile since the persons concerned may move to other posts. Formal collaborative arrangements are also necessary to create the kind of structures and facilities learners need in order to move from one learning environment or programme to another.

In recent years there has been a strong shift towards partnerships in providing education, training and support to people currently excluded from formal systems of education and employment. A range of collaborative arrangements have been forged in response to policy initiatives, funding requirements and local circumstances. The development of widening participation and lifelong learning partnerships and a plethora of other arrangements set up to achieve the aims of Government, such as the New Deal, Employment and Education Action zones, and the University for Industry, all require collaboration and partnerships between local agencies and providers, as do funding sources such as City Challenge, the Single Regeneration Budget and European Social Fund programmes. According to one community educator: *'no bidding document that crosses your desk these days doesn't have the word "partnership" on it'*.

The nature of partnerships inevitably varies according to local circumstances and the purposes for which they are formed. It is not partnerships *per se* but how they are managed when funding is achieved that is important. The evidence from people working in local communities is that, in order to develop meaningful routes between informal and formal learning, partnerships require the involvement of all key local agencies, all of whom should be treated and respected as equal partners rather than just as names on a funding application. This means that more powerful and better-resourced partners should treat smaller contributors with fairness and respect: *'It is vital that the expertise and approaches to learning adopted by all partners are respected and valued by network members.'* (Scottish Office, 1996: 4.9). Information provided for this study suggests that this is not always the case. In one locality visited, tenants' and residents' associations working with a local authority on community regeneration initiatives (including education) found that they were 'blocked' and shut out of decision-making once the grant money they had jointly applied for was obtained.

According to the evidence from the UK and elsewhere, the partnerships that are most effective in developing progression routes are those which have:

- Identified the strengths, resources and skills of each partner and what each can contribute.
- Arrived at agreement and shared understanding of goals, ways of working and quality assurance procedures.
- Secured some stability of funding.
- Developed mutual trust, openness and transparency in all dealings.
- Guaranteed continuity of membership and commitment of all partners.
- Secured the representation of user groups.
- Established clear communication channels and reporting structures.
- Established a clear set of tasks and concentrated efforts on achieving agreed priorities.

Partnership models

A variety of partnerships initiated to increase opportunities for local communities are already successfully operating. Different models include: specific local learning partnerships where education and training providers collaborate with the aim of 'joining up' or rationalising provision (eg. in Birmingham); partnerships that link education and community regeneration (eg. the *Coalfields Learning Initiatives Partnership*), and county-wide or regional partnerships to widen participation and provide progression opportunities (Open College Networks and access consortia).

5 Provision and curricular strategies

Targeted learning opportunities

The evidence collected for this study suggests that informal learning initiatives that are tailored to specific groups are often more effective in achieving upward educational progression than undifferentiated provision. A good example of this is informal provision targeted at women. As some of the earlier examples have demonstrated, many women embark on a learning path as a result of opportunities being provided in local environments with crèche or playgroup facilities. Women are also attracted back into learning when their children become less dependent and when they are looking for new directions in their lives. Informal opportunities provided in familiar local locations often act as stimuli to further learning for women who are at this life stage.

Many women also start on a learning pathway when their children start school. The desire to help children to achieve is a prime motivation for adults who join family learning schemes and literacy workshops. Some of these have resulted in impressive rates of subsequent progression as demonstrated in the examples below:

Schemes for parents

In 1995-96, **Parentscope** – a Parents Learning Network – was run in Birmingham as part of the community education service, with schools providing staff time, premises and materials. The aims were to encourage closer relationships between primary schools and parents; to promote greater parental involvement in children's education; to help both children and their parents to develop their knowledge and skills and to help adults into education, training, jobs and community activities.

The programme focused on adults as parents (courses on parenting, reading workshops and family literacy); parents as adults (Return to Learning, Aerobics, IT, Maths and First Aid); and parents as school helpers (parent-helper courses, play training, crèche worker training).

When evaluated in 1996, the scheme had, during a six month period, run 31 family workshops in 15 schools involving 526 parents; 12 first aid courses at 12 schools involving 100 adults; 8 English and maths courses at 6 schools for 55 adults; and 6 computer courses for 30 adults and two sign language courses involving 28, at one school. From any of these learning activities parents could, when they were ready, move on to other accredited programmes in the schools, adult education centres or colleges. These included RSA CLAIT, City and Guilds Word Power and Number Power, NVQ Levels 2 and 3 in Childcare and GCSE Maths. In developing these access and progression routes, the Community Education development officer was able to draw both on FEFC funding through the Adult Education budget, and Single Regeneration Budget/Challenge Fund money which enabled development of non formal activities and courses free from FEFC constraints.

Parentscope has now been absorbed within the City Council family support strategy and has evolved into the **Inspire** (Involving School Parents in Reading) programme (which also includes some numeracy work). This has retained a whole-school approach to bringing parents into schools and involving them in a partnership with their children's teachers. Funding for reading workshops and family literacy comes from the Core Skills Partnership (itself funded from SRB/Challenge) and the Standards Fund. Other courses are supported and delivered by local education and training providers. Schools themselves continue to provide premises, cover and gift time.

Recruitment

80 schools were contacted in 1997-98 and between 33 and 90 per cent of parents in these now regularly attend reading workshops or family literacy sessions. Two categories of parents tend to become involved: those who are not actively involved with the school but are attracted by reading workshops as a way of helping their children, and those who are already actively involved with the school as volunteer helpers.

It is found that parents respond better to a personal approach and targeting each class at a time or particular groups of children is more effective than open invitations to the whole school. Those who join reading or family literacy workshops are invited personally via the child. Certain times are seen as key intervention points for involving parents: induction meetings for incoming reception children, transitions between key stages, changes in teaching staff.

In recruiting and working with parents, a very sensitive approach is required, as witnessed during a visit to the school at the time of an introductory session. Those who have not been involved in post-school education or training often need verbal reassurances that any deficiencies in their knowledge and skills will not be exposed; that activities will be easy, enjoyable and non-threatening; that sessions will be informal and flexible and other members of the family can join in if desired.

Once involved, parents quickly lose any initial nervousness and start to enjoy working with their child. The reading workshops employ an informal and practical approach, offering simple ideas for parents to work with but also allowing the space for greater creativity as appropriate.

Outcomes

According to the co-ordinator, the programme has significantly raised achievement levels among children. It has also raised the confidence, skills and aspiration levels of many parents. She attributes this to its informality and relevance to their interests and motivations:

> 'The approach is come and help your child. They are essentially concerned about their own particular child and her/his progress and motivated by gaining something for them. They like to have opportunities for interacting with their child's teachers in informal, non-threatening ways and they like the semi-structured context in which to relate to other parents and children'.

Examples of schools involved in the programme:

Cotteridge School works together with a community project and the adult education service in providing learning activities for parents. As well as family reading workshops, family literacy and parent-helper sessions (for dinner supervisors), these have included courses in first aid, childcare (with NVQs), computers and maths courses. Parents are guided in their progression choices by a guidance worker based at Allenscroft Community Project.

A number of parents, the majority with no or few previous qualifications, have returned to learning through the programme. Some have started with Family Literacy and others with other learning areas. The following examples from the school demonstrate how reading workshops in schools can set many people on an educational pathway:

A participated in the reading workshop and Basic First Aid course; then did NVQ 2 and 3 in Childcare courses and a Back to Employment course. She became a voluntary dinner supervisor at Cotteridge School and a crèche organiser in another school

B moved from the reading workshop to a Basic First Aid Course. She then did City and Guilds Word Power and Number Power, NVQ 2 in childcare, a Back to Employment course and NVQ 3 in Childcare. She is now a voluntary dinner supervisor and part-time integration assistant at the school.

C who is a dinner supervisor at Cotteridge School went from the reading workshop to Basic First Aid, City and Guilds Number Power, Family Literacy, NVQ 2 in Childcare, voluntary work in the school's nursery school and NVQ 3 in Childcare.

D participated consecutively in the reading workshop; RSA computer course, Children's Games workshop, Basic First Aid, City and Guilds Word Power, O Level English, O Level maths, A Level English and computing course.

E, a school dinner supervisor, went on from the reading workshop to join courses in Family Literacy, First Aid, Childcare (NVQ 2), and Word Processing. She also took RSA CLAIT at Selly Oak College and a Back to Employment course as well as engaging in voluntary work in Cotteridge Nursery School.

F participated in the reading workshop, RSA computer course, Basic First Aid, Children's Games workshop, Aromatherapy, City and Guilds Word Power, City and Guilds Number Power. She then enrolled in courses in Advanced English and Advanced Computing at Fircroft College.

G went from the reading workshop to take courses in Basic First Aid, RSA CLAIT, Children's Games workshop, Aromatherapy, City and Guilds Word Power, City and Guilds Number Power. She also went on to take Advanced English and Advanced computing at Fircroft College.

H participated in the reading workshop than did NVQ 2 and NVQ 3 in Childcare and Basic First Aid. She is now a full-time classroom assistant at the school.

I participated in the reading workshop, First Aid, NVQ 2 and NVQ 3 in Childcare. She has become an Integration Assistant at another school and is now full-time Classroom Assistant at Cotteridge School.

J went on from the reading workshop to take courses in First Aid, City and Guilds Word Power and Number Power and Aromatherapy taster and course. She then enrolled in an Access to higher education programme at Fircroft College.

K went from the reading workshop to First Aid and RSA computing courses. She then took a computing course at an FE College and subsequently enrolled in an Arts Degree.

· · ·

At **Stirchley School** a similar process takes place: parents become engaged in learning through reading workshops and courses for school helpers which stimulate them to attend courses in other subjects. At this school, recruitment to the reading and parent helper workshops is assisted by a key individual who is variously a parent, a volunteer helper, a school governor a and member of the Parents and Teachers Association. She is enthusiastic about the scheme and acts as an important conduit of information as well as a role model to other parents.

Details supplied show that parents who are volunteer lunch-time supervisors frequently participate in the short courses and Reading Workshop, move from there to an Access to Classroom Assistants course and from there into certificated courses, with many gaining NVQs in Childcare, RSA Levels 1 and 2 in computers, Word and Number Power certificates and certificates in First Aid. Some have subsequently enrolled in A level courses in formal education institutions. As at Cotteridge School, first aid and computer courses have proved popular next learning steps (although First Aid is no longer offered as a result of the FEFC decision to fund only first aid at work courses).

Key features of the Birmingham parent-school partnership model which assist in widening participation and progression are:

- Supportive head teachers.
- Supportive individuals (teaching staff, development workers, parent volunteers) who inform, encourage and advise parents.
- Familiar, comfortable and non-threatening premises.
- The provision of some dedicated 'adult' space in a school.
- Offering parents other learning possibilities while they are still 'fired up' to learn.

According to the co-ordinator, learning programmes for parents need to be seen as a part of routine school activities, something that people expect to be available and are expected to come to: *'In many schools it has become an anticipated event each year or each term'.*
(Source: visits to Cotteridge and Stirchley Schools and information supplied by Beryl Bateson, Birmingham Education Department; Chris Rose, Birmingham City Council; Kate Basterfield, Stirchley Primary School).

Long-term unemployed adults

The Churches Initiative on Training, Employment and Enterprise (CITEE) was set up in 1989 by churches across Coventry to address the needs of unemployed people who were not being catered for by existing organisations and initiatives. The central aim was to help this group to regain the confidence, motivation and personal skills required to be successful in the workplace.

CITEE operates in a church hall and helps long-term and frequently unemployed people from all over Coventry. Many have disabilities or special learning needs and are referred by Social Services, Health Services and other agencies. Some are ex-offenders and people with alcohol or drug dependency. They are offered the possibility of joining an informal course, funded by Coventry City Council Economic Development Division, entitled *A Foot in the Door*. The ten-week programme is run several times a year for groups of up to 10 people. The course is free, bus fares are reimbursed and refreshments are provided. The courses tend to attract a majority of men with an average age of about 34.

The course is concerned with developing personal and social skills rather than specialised work skills. Essential components are confidence-building, job search, interview skills, action planning and short work tasters in a variety of organisational contexts. Reading and writing elements are kept to a minimum. Outings and social occasions, such as a Christmas party and celebrations at the beginning and end of courses, are built into the programme, with trainees encouraged to do all the planning and arranging. This helps to develop skills such as negotiating, organising, budgeting and working as a team, with trainers playing an advisory and feedback role. Teamwork is considered a vital element of the course and trainees sign a group contract, on arrival, on the responsibilities of working together as a team.

Although structured, the course also has the flexibility to respond to any requirements and interests expressed by the group. There is a strong focus on helping individuals to progress. At the end of the course, all participants receive a folder containing a completion certificate, a promise of continuing support, copies of their CV, a flow chart with steps to gaining a job, a personal action plan drawn up with the help of the group; a list of useful addresses and contacts to help them find employment; reminders about interview skills and a group testimonial containing positive things said about them by other members of the group. After the course trainees receive continuing support from drop-in facilities and post-training support workers.

According to a report on the 12th Programme, all participants felt it had helped them grow in confidence, find more direction in their lives and develop skills that would help them find and use in employment. Five were planning to do voluntary work while looking for paid employment; two were taking courses in English, maths and computer skills provided elsewhere; another was applying to do an English course at a college and was also intending to do some voluntary work; one had been offered work on a trial basis at the firm where he had done a work taster and another had *'significantly changed his lifestyle which had previously been almost entirely nocturnal'*.

These are typical outcomes and the factors that contribute to them are:

- The informal, supportive and friendly environment
- Staff encouragement, counselling and support
- Responsiveness to interests and needs
- Provision of work tasters
- Specific help with progression routes
- Provision of post training support.

(Source: McGivney and Thomson, 1995)

Asian women

Nav-Yug Asian Women's Project was established in Coventry in 1991 to meet the needs of Asian women, a particularly disadvantaged section of the city's population with an unemployment rate almost twice as high as that of white women in the city. Housed in informal surroundings in a community college, the scheme provides social and self-help opportunities, informal recreational classes, vocational and semi-vocational training. Learning activities are set up in response to identified needs and have included English for Speakers of Other languages (ESOL), Information Technology, Sewing, Fashion Design, Confidence Building, Interview Skills, Enterprise training and Keep Fit. There is also a weekly drop-in facility to provide information, guidance and counselling.

The project provides follow-on courses where possible and it is found that virtually all of the women who participate in ESOL proceed onto other courses: '*Once a course finishes they look for other courses. Prior to the arrival of the project, only about 5 per cent of participants in the adult education classes on site were from minority groups; now the proportion is 26 per cent*'.

A focus group conducted with current and former participants found that several had gone from *Nav-Yug* courses to take a BTEC course in Nursery Nursing at a college; one had gone to a college to take a City and Guilds qualification in translating and interpreting; another had become a sewing tutor and was taking GCSE courses; another was following a two-year course in Business Administration at a college. Over half of the women who had taken the enterprise course had subsequently enrolled in further education programmes. There were also several examples of women moving into employment and self-employment:

- An ESOL tutor, who had originally come as a volunteer to help women learn English, subsequently took a teaching qualification and had established a teaching career both at *Nav-Yug* and in other education and training establishments.
- A woman who had joined an ESOL class and, subsequently, the enterprise course had set up her own clothing business.
- A woman who had moved from an ESOL class to the enterprise course then to an RSA Business Enterprise course had become a part-time tutor at a school
- Some former and current trainees had returned as volunteer ESOL tutors

A particularly important outcome of the informal learning activities was that participants were likely to have significantly more contact and involvement with their children's schools. In 1995, their attendance at school events such as parents' evenings had increased from 5 to 50 per cent.

The following were perceived as key factors in helping the women to progress:

- Location: The project is in an area with a large Asian community and is sited at the local community college which combines a school and adult education centre. This means Asian women can bring their children to school and attend learning activities on the same site in a non-threatening venue with a friendly and informal atmosphere.
- Cultural sensitivity. The project takes account of the different cultural backgrounds of Asian women and is for women only. (Many Asian women could not attend mixed ESOL classes.)
- Responsiveness. Courses and facilities are tailored to interests and needs identified by Asian women.
- Support. Courses are free and there is a crèche.
- Asian staff. Staff and volunteers are from the same community and fluent in both English and Asian languages
- Encouraging and supportive staff.
- Mutually supportive learning groups: '*We help each other and learn from each other.*' *We learn a lot from others as well as tutors*'
- Provision of some courses at different levels allowing progression
- Links with other education providers, particularly community education.

(Source: McGivney and Thomson, 1995)

People recovering from mental illness

Park Lane College in Leeds has been running an informal non-accredited programme – **Bring out the Best in Yourself** – for people recovering from mental illness. These take place in day centres in collaboration with centre managers. The learning involves small groups and covers areas such as stress management and conflict resolution: *'The "what" isn't important. It's the process of proving that they can still learn, this improves their self-esteem'.*

When they are ready, groups are encouraged to visit a local education centre where they are introduced to other learning programmes and different tutors: *'It's a huge leap for them to move to another site where there are other people and other activities but they have common reference points with their own group and own tutor'.* Moving together in small groups provides familiarity and support.

As a result of the gradual progression process, some individuals have gone into full-time courses and employment. One has enrolled in courses in listening and accredited counselling skills and some now themselves work as volunteers with mentally recovering people.
(Source: Park Lane College)

All of these examples are of provision that has been carefully targeted at specific groups, with progression options provided for those who wish to continue learning. A key point is that progression to other levels and types of learning is only encouraged when individuals or groups are perceived to be ready for this. Referring people on too early can be counter-productive and either frighten people off or put them in a position where they risk failure.

Provision of 'safe' learning options

The focus of the first informal learning experience frequently has little bearing on an individual's future learning trajectory. People often choose familiar, non-threatening or stereotypical learning activities as a starting point and participation in these gives them the confidence to progress to something quite different. Providing 'safe' first learning options has therefore been found a useful strategy for widening participation and helping people to develop other learning interests. An outreach guidance worker in the Forest of Dean has found that informal craft-related programmes often act as an effective starting point in a learning pathway: *'People are often scared of academic things and do crafts because they think it's easier. They then branch out into other thing.'* Some participants in these have subsequently moved on to the FEFC-funded City and Guilds course *'Learning Support in Community Settings'.* This programme is popular because it is relevant, practical and related to local employment opportunities: *'If you're looking for a job in this area, caring is one of the main possibilities'.* The course has a work placement element and the majority of participants subsequently obtain employment. Others have gone on to take programmes in Basic Skills, Makaton, British Sign Language and teacher training.

The guidance worker has also found that informal crafts programmes have their own progression outcomes. She gave several examples of the process:

In the **Forest of Dean** two women who had joined informal craft courses in a neighbourhood setting went on to develop a craft guild, mostly made up of other members of the learning group. They eventually opened their own shop.

A woman who had taken a course in Sugarcraft in an Opportunity Centre (a community facility for pre-school children and their families) went on to take a City and Guilds professional catering course at the local college and has since started her own business selling confectionery.

A woman with young twins who started by learning Sugarcraft in a family centre moved on to take courses in flower arranging, hairdressing and catering at the local college. She subsequently established a complete wedding service offering all these services as well as professional make-up provided by her daughter who had been trained in beauty. (Source: Royal Forest of Dean College)

Provision of a range of learning opportunities in the same local setting

Many people who have returned to learning in the community need time before they are ready or prepared to attend a formal educational environment. For many it is too big a leap to go straight from informal learning in the community into a formal education institution. Thus some tutors have found that, in order to prevent learners from repeating courses at the same level in an environment they are reluctant to leave, they need to provide intermediate level programmes to increase their confidence and prepare them for more advanced courses. The *Nav Yug* project which provides informal learning opportunities for Asian women always tries to put on courses at a slightly higher level: *'to build on the steps taken. It is not always possible for women to go elsewhere. It can be too big a jump to go straight onto college courses which women find too difficult'.* (McGivney and Thomson, 1995)

The evidence indicates that the provision of both informal and formal learning opportunities in the same setting often encourages people who would not have considered approaching an education institution to enrol in more formal programmes. Community education workers have found that the offer of different types of learning in the same venue allows people to move easily from one to the other. One suggested that community education providers should always have help with basic skills available as people who engage in informal learning often reach a point where they need it: *'You should have some basic skills potential available because sooner or later the penny will drop and they'll realise they need to be able to write things'*. He likened the best community learning service to a carousel on which there are community development opportunities, informal learning possibilities and formal learning possibilities:

We ought to encourage people to get on the carousel at the point that they find most comfortable. We need to recognise that they need to change seats from time to time. It is never just in one direction. If people feel empowered in one arena, they feel empowered in other arenas. We still have an ABE (adult basic education) unit here. Some of the most vocal and powerful people here started off as ABE students. That empowerment opened up other areas for them. It's quite easy to facilitate crossover between formal and informal here because of the scale of our work. We have a whole range of opportunities here and a whole range of workers – a critical mass of informal stuff to balance the formal, and people here have a multiplicity of roles. There's a family nutrition project and community education worker working with Adult Basic Education on pregnancy testing.'

Basic skills

Basic skills provision can be an important entry point for disadvantaged individuals. However, many do not come forward for help out of fear of stigma. When integrated with areas of interest and concern to individuals – local issues, children's progress, practical activities, First Aid, form filling, Highway Code, etc – literacy is not seen as the prime objective and therefore protects people from the feelings of shame or inadequacy they might feel if activities were presented as purely focused on basic skills.

Linked provision

Movement between learning programmes provided in different locations is facilitated when there are explicit links between them.

> **The WEA** is trying to link all provision so that learners can move with ease between different types of learning programme. The Association is developing a system whereby many of the courses it provides are connected in a way that creates learning pathways. The idea is to enable learners to move freely and in any direction between courses, whether 'liberal', targeted, accredited or non-accredited, avoiding strict 'vertical' definitions of progression.
>
> The development of the system requires some collaboration with partner organisations and the WEA has been increasingly working in partnership with trade unions, charities, local authorities and other education providers to develop and deliver programmes that respond to the needs of learners. The system involves built-in progression: *'Attention is paid always to the potential for continued study at the end of a course and addresses the issue of "what next?" so that students can build upon their initial successes and maintain their commitment to learning'.* (WEA, 1998a: 7)

Curricular strategies

There are a number of curricular mechanisms which help learners to move between different learning levels and environments: incremental programmes with a foundation or introductory course followed by courses at progressively more advanced levels; exploratory Return to Learn courses which include guidance and expose people to a range of options; taster courses which provide short samples of programmes to enable people to make an informed choice; bridging courses that assist transition between different learning environments and levels; modular programmes enabling people to take parts of a programme at different times and, if necessary, in different places; accredited programmes such as access programmes leading to higher level study.

Providing courses in subjects at several levels, as, for example, in modern languages, is an obvious strategy for promoting progression. In the London Borough of Harrow, the majority of subjects in the LEA adult non-Schedule 2 programme are presented in several stages: an introductory level; continuation, and sometimes a third stage. There have also been efforts to make the skills appropriate for each level more explicit and to negotiate individual learning goals with all learners. (Adkins, 1997)

Access routes

Access routes are also very important in assisting educational progression and these have been found to be particularly popular with women and people from ethnic minority communities. Access Validating Agencies (AVAs) (many of which are also Open College Networks) validate Access to higher education programmes within a framework of credits and levels. They are authorised to award 'Kitemarked' Access to higher education certificates for the achievement of a minimum of 16 credits through planned programmes of study at levels appropriate to entry to HE.

For many people, however, Access courses are not the first step in a learning pathway but the second or third, and it is often found that students embarking on such programmes have previously undertaken informal learning in the community which has given them the confidence and motivation to enrol in an access, return to learn or other form of bridging course (McGivney, 1992).

Making your experience count

Programmes that aim to help learners recognise their experience, talents and potential often motivate people to undertake other learning programmes. Surveys of outcomes for learners who had participated in *Make Your Experience Count* courses in Somerset in 1991 and 1993 showed that 87 per cent and 72 per cent of participants respectively had gone on to take a community education or college course; 58 per cent and 46 per cent had found a part-time job and 11 per cent/3 per cent, a full-time job (information from Somerset Community Education).

Cocktail funding

Those who are providing informal learning opportunities with progression options in the community have usually succeeded in drawing down funding from different sources such as Europe, the Further Education Funding Council, Single Regeneration Budget (SRB) and non-Schedule 2 in order to mount different levels of learning provision. The Linwood community education centre on Saffron Estate in Leicester, for example, receives funding from the local authority, FEFC and the Lottery and is able to provide both informal and formal learning opportunities, including Adult Basic Education, on the same premises.

'Cocktail' funding, involving several funding sources, facilitates progression. European, non-Schedule 2 and SRB funding enables targeted first-step provision, taster courses and small groups as well as support for things like travel and childcare. FEFC-funded provision allows providers to offer accredited, vocational and higher level opportunities.

6 Accreditation

The recording of achievement for any form or level of learning can significantly motivate people by increasing their confidence and compensating for any earlier 'failure'. It can also encourage continuing learning and increase demand for progression opportunities. Achievements can be recorded through national or 'home grown' accreditation systems, the National Record of Achievement or a Progress File.

Many education providers who offer learning opportunities in the community try and link these with accredited routes for those who want them. The most common and popular form of accreditation for community-based learners is Open College Network accreditation. The evidence suggests that other frequently used accreditation routes (depending on specific needs and subject areas) are City and Guilds Word Power and Number Power and Learning Support in Community Settings; RSA CLAIT; and NVQs in areas such as child care. Many informal learners also progress to academic programmes such as GCSE in English or Maths.

As the following example illustrates, progression along these routes often depends on the raising of confidence at the earlier learning level, the encouragement and support of 'key' individuals or agencies, and the availability of the accredited programmes in the same setting or near locality.

Park Lane College has developed a **Caring in the Community Framework** – a programme that is offered in range of informal centres across the city and targeted at people working in a caring capacity: among others, childminders, playscheme workers, volunteer helpers in schools, and those caring for the elderly or people with disabilities and learning difficulties.

The programme is flexible and modular. There are four core areas and the rest are negotiated with groups to meet needs. There is optional Open College accreditation and this has proved a significant aid to progression: 'The first level teaches them about accreditation, how to put together a portfolio and a learning diary, showing how they are using what they are doing in other contexts such as the home. It's a gentle introduction to accreditation – the beginnings of reflection which can lead them into Level 2'.

The programme is also integrated with ABE and ESOL frameworks and outcomes have been devised to meet funding requirements for these.

Potential progression routes are varied (there are 29 options) and both vertical and horizontal. The programme can lead to jobs, accreditation to Level 3 and qualifications such as City and Guilds 7321/01 (Learning Support in the Community) or NVQs in Playwork or Childcare, offered at the main college site or elsewhere. Alternatively, it can lead to another Level 2 to consolidate learning at that level. Exit guidance is incorporated in the programme and during the last of the ten-week sessions, a guidance worker joins the group to discuss possible directions. She also provides individual guidance on request.

Between 1996 and 1998 enrolments on the programme totalled around 400 each year with the vast majority of participants achieving accreditation.

During a visit to the Crossgates Centre, a short meeting was held with a group of ten Level 3 students, all women, most of whom were support assistants in schools. Some had come from a neighbouring ward. For people to move across neighbourhood boundaries in this area was considered to be significant progression in itself.

The women's main reason for starting the programme was the desire to work with children and keep up with what their children were doing at school. Some had enrolled because they had heard about the course from friends or other school support workers. Most had already done Levels 1 and 2 and several spoke about the momentum that had built up from their first informal step back into learning:

> 'Once you've made the move it's like being on a bus: you want to keep moving';
> 'There's a snowball effect: your confidence builds and you want to do more'.

The women's comments suggested that there has been a 'cascade' effect from their learning as they are acting as role models to their families and friends. The mother of one participant had started a course and others had friends who were interested in doing something similar. Several had also found their children more motivated to learn: *'I'm at little school and mum's at big school'*.

The success of the *Framework* programme in widening participation and encouraging progression is attributed to the following features:
- Delivery in local venues which means that students are able to attend on their familiar territory (the college has 60 adult education centres in the community and courses can also be run in specific venues such as schools and playschemes).
- The informal style of the programme: *'Sometimes people not really aware they're on a "course"'*.
- Learning that is relevant to people's lives and interests: *'People see what they are doing as relevant to their interests not education in the abstract. Suddenly seeing that education can be relevant is a huge leap'*.
- Programmes that are flexible and negotiated.
- Flexible timing (two hours a week for ten weeks or four hours a week for five weeks, which is considered an easy commitment).
- Short, manageable 'bite-sized' courses.
- Optional Open College accreditation.
- Having something to show for what has been learned (a portfolio; credits).
- Provision of guidance.
- Student support (for example, dyslexic students can receive one-to-one support from students on Tutor Training placements; some one-to-one tutorials can be provided in the home).
- Fee waivers for people in certain categories and low fees for those who are low waged.
- The free crèche.
- Consistency of quality (quality assurance is achieved through Open College internal and external moderators and the college's own quality system).

(Source: Celia Moorhouse, Jill Kibble and staff and students at Crossgates Learning Centre)

For those wishing to progress to more advanced levels of study without this kind of support, the range and complexity of qualifications available can be intimidating and confusing:

The jungle of available awards leads to confusion about the currency value and equivalence of qualifications and risks undermining learners' achievements in the eyes of employers and other interested parties. (WEA, 1998b: 22)

The Qualifications and Curriculum Authority (QCA) is addressing this situation and one of the aims is to create a greater potential for pathways between vocational and academic routes.

Credit frameworks

Many believe that there is an urgent need to accredit achievements as distinct from courses, and there is widespread support for a coherent national credit framework which would allow funding bodies, learners and employers to recognise the value of all qualifications. There is also substantial support for unitisation which would enable achievements to be described, measured and valued in the same way across all qualifications.

Few areas of education have produced such unanimity. The Kennedy Widening Participation Committee, the National Advisory Group for Continuing Education and Lifelong Learning, the National Committee of Enquiry into Higher Education and the Further Education Funding Council have all separately argued for a national credit framework, and in 1998, a joint statement issued by the National Credit Framework Strategic Advisory Group, which includes representatives from all education sectors and national vocational awarding bodies, called for a credit-based qualifications system which would enable funding to be based on credit rather than *'the mode-based approach of full- and part-time attendance which is becoming increasingly outdated given the diversity of learning patterns'*.

The consensus on the need for a national credit framework cuts across regions and education sectors. The Further Education Funding Council is committed to the development of a unit-based credit framework and linked funding methodology, and is currently conducting a small-scale unitisation funding pilot. In Wales where the further education system is already funded by credit, the system is being extended to higher education and will be phased in for all taught courses by 2002. The Inter-Consortium Credit Agreement (InCCA) Project, involving three credit consortia in England and Wales, has produced a report, *A Common Framework for Learning*, (September 1998) strongly supporting the principles of a single unified framework.

A new credit and qualifications framework has also been announced in Scotland. The new scheme builds on SCOTCAT – the credit-transfer scheme supported by all Scottish higher education institutions – and will produce a framework covering all Scottish qualifications wherever gained.

The WEA (1998b) believes that a national credit accumulation and transfer system should be developed alongside a credit framework. The Association argues that such a system should be underpinned by robust monitoring mechanisms and supported by high quality guidance and advice to learners ensuring that appropriate choices are made from the range of opportunities available. The WEA has developed its own mechanism allowing learners to transfer credits across districts for particular accredited programmes.

A credit framework is particularly appropriate for adults who are obliged by circumstances to learn in a discontinuous and intermittent way. It also suits people with no or few qualifications and little experience of post-school education as it allows small achievements to be recognised. Some of the most successful programmes designed for adult learners, such as Open College Network accredited courses, Access courses and Return to Study programmes, are credit-based.

Open College Networks (OCNs)

Open College Networks have developed a model of a unitised, credit-based system which is particularly suited to people who return to learn informally in the community. The system allows achievements to be expressed in terms of learning outcomes organised into units. Individuals can present evidence of their achievements (including prior learning acquired in different environments) in relation to these outcomes and claim credit for successful completion of the units. A single definition of credit is applied to all learning achievements. Credits are not classified, graded, sub-divided or labelled so there is parity of esteem. Moreover the accreditation is voluntary. This is particularly important for people who initially lack confidence. People can engage in an OCN-accredited programme without taking credit. Alternatively, they can opt into credit during the course of the programme; they can take a single credit (it does not have to be part of work towards a qualification); or they can work towards part or the whole of a qualification.

Another aspect of the OCN system that particularly suits community-based learning is that the process is flexible and customised to requirements. Target groups have to be clearly identified and programmes designed specifically to meet their needs. As each new programme has to be recognised and validated by a panel of peers, quality is maintained. For example, one OCN-accredited area is training for volunteers and workers in voluntary organisations. The accredited units have not been developed centrally but have developed in accordance with the requirements of people in voluntary organisations around the country. The National Open College Network (NOCN) is now trying to bring it all within the framework of a qualification. According to a college outreach worker in Leeds: *'OCN accreditation has been superb for us working in the community: they are flexible, can be customised and responsive'*.

Family Centres in Gloucestershire have produced their own Open College Network accredited units in areas such as parenting, healthy living, creative arts, welfare rights, citizenship, art and glass painting. Some of these offer national OCN units. The aims are to offer a range of accredited opportunities for parents and carers and other users of the centres; to reintroduce them to education and training; and to increase their confidence and to encourage them to participate in education and training.

According to the National Open College Network (NOCN), OCN accreditation has achieved a much higher profile in recent years. This is partly attributed to a multiplier effect: seeing some people achieve credits motivates others to want them. FEFC data show that OCNs are collectively the largest single awarding body for adult learners in the further education sector. In 1997-98, OCN accreditation was offered through 2,900 centres and the largest single group of providers using the accreditation were voluntary organisations (800).

The flexibility of OCN accreditation makes it particularly attractive to informal learners, especially those who have benefited least from education in the past. Research conducted for the WEA (Cordon, 1993) found that OCN accreditation was *'surprisingly popular'* among those undertaking return to learn programmes. The value it places on learning achieved in non-educational contexts such as the home, the workplace or the community boosts confidence and increases motivation to learn. In 1996-97, 62 per cent of registrations on OCN-accredited programmes were women; 16 per cent were members of ethnic minority groups; 18 per cent were unemployed and 31 per cent unwaged. It is also estimated that over 50 per cent of learners following basic education and English as a Second Language courses are on OCN accredited-programmes.

Progression routes

OCN accreditation encourages learner progression by providing a framework of levels from entry level to level 4, through which learners can progress at their own pace. There is also a new pre-foundation level. This has been developed to prepare learners for foundation programmes. It includes guidance, key skills and optional units tailored to the needs of specific groups such as learners with literacy and numeracy needs, underachieving school pupils or learners with moderate learning difficulties.

The levels provide clear progression routes and the awards achieved, being part of a national accreditation network, can be recognised as equivalents to national qualifications such as GCSE and NVQ.

OCN accreditation also assists education progression by encouraging cross-sectoral and inter-institutional collaboration and planning within the networks. This enables articulation between different systems and allows learners to move from local, targeted and less formal provision into more formal, mainstream provision. A study of the effect of OCN accreditation on learner motivation and progression (FEU, 1993) found that in one Federation, 33 per cent of learners with credits from three different programmes had gained them in more than one sector and had moved between further education, adult education, voluntary, community or employer-based provision. The biggest group – 19 per cent – had moved from adult education into further education. The study also showed that the accreditation was particularly useful to learners from the black community, women, those with no or low level qualifications and people in lower socio-economic groups. The majority of respondents, particularly those who were black, female or over the age of 35, said that the credits had helped to boost their confidence and increase their ambitions. 72 per cent of all respondents had either progressed to another course or continued their current learning programme after completing their accredited course. The research as a whole demonstrated that:

- OCN-accredited programmes were recruiting groups who are traditionally under-represented in education and training.
- Learners joined courses for a range of personal, social, educational and vocational motives.
- During the course of the learning programme, learners' confidence was boosted, and their ambitions and expectations raised.
- Most, including those who had no original intention or ambition to do so, had undertaken further learning.
- Most respondents associated credits with enhanced value, higher quality, and increased recognition by others. (FEU, 1993; Mager, 1993)

More recent research (Capizzi, 1999) found that OCN accreditation was valued very positively by participants in TUC programmes for union workplace and health and safety representatives. The study revealed *'exceptionally'* high rates of participation, achievement and award of credits. Within the London Open College Network, for example, 97 per cent of representatives were awarded credit. For over 20 per cent of all participants this was the first nationally recognised certification and the accreditation enabled many people to see themselves as successful learners for the first time. It also encouraged participants to be more positive about their own abilities and to participate in further education and training (although future learning plans were exclusively related to union and TUC provision). The study notes that the accredited courses gave participants access not only to further opportunities for education and training but also to *'a language for mapping skills and knowledge – whether achievements or needs'*. It was also found that accreditation had enhanced the quality of the course without distorting the ethos of purposes of programmes.

Other examples of progression from OCN programmes are given in Appendix 1.

There is substantial evidence, therefore, that OCN accreditation is very popular among those learning in the community and often leads to educational progression. Some practitioners, however, believe that NVQs are more effective in vocational progression (helping people to find jobs) as many employers do not recognise OCN awards. Other have found OCN units to be variable in quality:

OCNs tend to be seen as a local thing. The voluntary sector is more likely to recognise OCN credits. As far as employers are concerned, NVQs are more important. OCN credits are variable and therefore vary in the way they are perceived. (College outreach worker)

A possible problem with progression is that OCN credits are not yet universal currency. This is partly an issue to do with information: employers may be familiar with GCSEs and NVQs but often OCN credits are new to them. (...) There seems to be confusion among tutors, students and OCN development staff over questions of equivalence. (Blythe, 1999: 19)

Some of the people consulted during this study expressed anxieties about the potential impact on OCN accreditation of the regulatory framework for all qualifications being developed by the Qualifications and Curriculum Agency (QCA). The fear is that new requirements might remove some of the essential features of OCN accreditation – namely its flexibility and ability to customise provision. This would have an extremely negative effect on the system's ability to respond to community learning needs as well as weakening its position in the national qualification system. These anxieties have also been expressed in the study of accredited TUC provision.

Despite the wide achievements of the Open College Networks in increasing and widening adult participation and the types of programmes available, it can be argued that the OCNs are vulnerable and the OCN ethos fragile. Any form of public funding for development of OCN-based provision has been negligible especially in comparison with the very significant funding and infrastructural support given to development and review of GNVQs whose impact in terms of student numbers is much less. The status and place of OCN credits in the national qualifications system remains problematic. The usefulness of 'credits' depends ultimately on the development of a national credit framework.

The vitality and creativity of course activities could be sapped by mooted pressures on or from the Qualifications and Curriculum Agency to privilege traditional techniques for achieving 'reliability' in assessment, rather than to promote and support systematic investigation and development of rigorous yet innovative techniques for ensuring the reliability of what is acknowledged as exceptionally valid methods of assessment. (Capizzi, 1999: 45)

This study suggests that any attempt to stifle the characteristic flexibility and responsiveness of the OCN accreditation process will have a detrimental effect on progression routes from community-based programmes. OCNs provide the most effective bridge that has yet been designed between different levels of learning and different learning environments. The TUC study quoted above found that the accreditation process simultaneously allows innovation and flexibility in programmes and ensures rigour and quality.

The appropriateness of accreditation

It is important to note that, despite the successes noted above, accreditation may not be appropriate for all adult learners. 37 per cent of respondents to a recent survey said that the current stress on qualifications had put them off learning (Campaign for Learning/MORI, 1998). If accreditation is mentioned or introduced too soon it can give rise to anxieties about failure. As Merton (1998) points out in relation to 'disaffected' young people, accreditation can be both a barrier as well as a motivator, awakening unpleasant memories of school assessment exams and previous academic failure. Similarly, the WEA (1998b: 23), while welcoming *The Learning Age*'s proposal to introduce new entry level or 'starter' qualifications, warns that, for some potential learners, the prospect of accreditation acts as a barrier to returning to study:

> *Formal accreditation is only one measure by which achievement is recognised. (. . .) For many adult learners the requirement of formal assessment is inappropriate. Previous poor educational experiences and examination failure can turn adults away from learning for life. Initiatives to encourage their return to study are often ineffective if the learning programme is required to focus primarily on achieving qualifications.*

During the course of this study a number of informants also questioned the wisdom and desirability of attaching accreditation to all learning programme. The following were typical comments from some of the outreach, guidance and community education workers consulted:

> *There's been a rush to accredit whether it's appropriate or not.*

> *There's a problem of 'shoehorning' programmes to make them accreditable. Key features [of informal learning programmes] should be flexibility and 'intentionality' on the part of the learner. Sometimes you have to have the courage to let learning lie.*

> *There's a question about fitting everything into a credit framework. It's not always appropriate and can create barriers. Not all learners are ready for or interested in accreditation.*

Strategies for identifying outcomes

Many people involved in providing learning for adults believe that a it is important to have more than one way of measuring and valuing learning achievements. The WEA, for example, has developed a Learning Outcome strategy which aims to recognise the: *'valuable levels of learning that take place in classes for which formal accreditation is considered by students as inappropriate'* (1998a: 7). The strategy encourages students to take greater responsibility for their own learning and to reflect on it and identify their learning achievements:

> *Tutors produce syllabuses that make the proposed learning outcomes of the course explicit, defining what students should be able to think, do, feel or say as a result of their newly acquired knowledge and understanding. These outcomes are discussed and agreed by the class and may be modified during the course. At the end of the course, students are encouraged to reflect upon their learning and consider how best to continue their studies.* (WEA, 1998a: 7)

An FEFC inspection report in 1995 stated that the learning outcomes strategy had produced clarity in objectives and schemes of work for each course and was helping students to consider their future progression routes (FEDA, 1997).

Some providers have introduced similar strategies within non-Schedule-2 provision. An example is given here:

In the **London Borough of Harrow**, the consortium of tertiary colleges has reviewed all non-Schedule 2 course materials to ensure that intended learning outcomes are sufficiently explicit. Courses are offered at two levels, introduction and continuation, and sometimes there is a third level. A record of achievement is available for learners taking courses of 30 hours' tuition or more who want to follow a progression pathway. This is jointly validated by the colleges and is voluntary, with the cost met by learners. Assessment is undertaken by the course tutor, backed up by moderation through a tutor at a different college. The record of achievement is available for LEA-sponsored programmes such as flower arranging, cake decoration, sugarcraft, dress and fashion and soft furnishings, and for subjects which students tend to repeat, sometimes for a number of years (yoga, sports classes, fitness/keep fit).

Another level of learning recognition that has been introduced is the Harrow Learners Award. The purpose is to recognise and reward significant achievement gained through participation in the LEA programme. A subject-based version is awarded to learners who have pursued a particular subject through several stages of progression, and another version is available for groups such as older people, and students with learning difficulties or disabilities. The award is made in response to application by the learner, with the endorsement of tutors. Assessment is by a panel of tutors. Awards are validated jointly by the three colleges and the London Borough of Harrow. (Adkins, 1997)

Assessment of prior learning

Reflection on prior learning, especially learning that has taken place in non-educational environments and contexts, contributes to motivation and educational progression.

Two main approaches to APEL (assessment or accreditation of prior experiential learning) have been identified: the 'credit exchange' model and the 'developmental' model (Butterworth, 1992). In the credit exchange model, credit is awarded for informal learning through a 'matching process' whereby individuals reflect on their experience and competencies and present evidence of prior learning in order to gain credit for an accredited programme. The developmental model involves an exploration of personal experience through means such as keeping a diary or writing a biography. The learner is required to evaluate previous experiences and demonstrate the learning derived both from them and the reflection process. However, the process need not lead to accreditation. It allows people to value their learning for itself, before deciding whether or not they want their learning assessed and accredited.

According to some reports (see: Fraser, 1995; Baillie *et al*, 1998), education institutions place more stress on the credit- and outcomes-based approach than on the developmental approach. This is viewed as a negative development as it obliges learners to identify and value only those types of learning and experience that meet the requirements of awarding bodies, institutions or employers. Some believe that the matching of learning experiences to predetermined outcomes downgrades the personal growth element that is an essential element in learner progression. They argue that the APEL process should not lead to accreditation unless it is appropriate for the individual learner:

Much of the potential for valuing the range of individual experience and finding creative outlets for its expression is being eroded as market forces increasingly hold sway over issues of vocational and educational relevance, and, by extension, of personal and social value (...) As long as recognition of the individual's learning process reigns within the heart and mind of the student, we can encourage the journey of discovery and applaud the outcome of increased self-esteem. But when students seek others' acknowledgements of the relevance of their new-found learning, for example to vocational or educational requirements, they must articulate that learning in a manner which will meet the approval of an external reader and assessor. Private concerns have become a matter for public adjudication. (Fraser, 1995: 138-139)

This raises one of the major issues relating to informal learning – how it is valued. The imposition of pre-determined standards and prescribed outcomes on something that is so diverse and personal can stifle the dynamic nature of individual learning and distort the process of self-discovery.

The value of reflecting on prior experience and identifying previous learning is that it gives people greater understanding of their learning and increases self-esteem. Many practitioners believe that individuals should be encouraged to manage their own learning experiences, to recognise where they start from, their preferred styles and modes of learning, and the time and opportunities they have for learning (Jessup, 1995). Guidance is an important means of helping them to do this.

7 The role of guidance in educational progression

For many people the existence of clear learning routes, defined by levels, accreditation or incremental programmes, may not be enough to set them on a continuing learning pathway. Successful transitions from informal to formal learning depend not only on the availability and accessibility of next-step programmes but also, and critically, on people's awareness of them. If a range of learning opportunities is offered in the same community venue, people are likely on the whole to know about them; if the next learning steps are provided in other learning environments, then people may not take advantage of them, because they are unaware of the programmes available, because they lack confidence, or because they have inaccurate or outdated ideas about education and education institutions. An essential prerequisite for educational progression is accurate information. However, information on its own is not always enough. People need to know what to do with it and how to use it. They need to be guided through the possibilities.

Although *Learning Direct* – the national telephone helpline – is a welcome innovation, there are some questions about the quality of advice that is offered. Moreover, as stressed by some of the community education and guidance workers reporting to this project, telephone guidance systems are not always appropriate for the people least represented in formal education and training: *'You need to be confident and organised in your thinking to ring a Helpline. Lots of people don't have a phone or are not comfortable speaking on phone.'* The most effective form of guidance for these individuals is an informal, one-to-one interaction. Munn, Tett and Arney (1993) identified different categories of adult learner: those who are motivated and have a clear understanding of their goals; those who are highly motivated but unclear about their goals and those who are more 'reluctant' learners. Each of these groups requires a different approach, and within each of them, every individual will have specific circumstances, interests and priorities that have a bearing on the directions they are able or prepared to take. Personal guidance can be pivotal in helping people to enter and progress along a learning pathway.

The importance of local information, advice and guidance services in complementing and supporting initiatives such as Learning Direct and the University for Industry has been acknowledged in *The Learning Age* (DfEE, 1998) and the Government has since allocated £54m over three years for local guidance provision. This will be funded through partnerships which will include community and voluntary groups. The new funding has been widely welcomed after a long period during which *'extant'* guidance services have had to survive: *'on uncertain, temporary and eccentric cocktails of funding'* (Brown, 1999: 7). There are, however, reservations about some of the proposals contained in the consultative document *Local Information and Advice and Guidance for adults in England: Towards a National Framework* (DfEE, 1999). The document proposes that all adults should have access to free information about learning opportunities, signposting to further information or guidance and, if necessary, a brief discussion with an adviser. There will also be free guidance interviews for New Deal and other targeted groups. This suggests that other adults, perhaps the majority, will have to pay for this service: *'the position for most adults is that they have to pay for guidance interviews. In other*

this. People's horizons are inevitably structured by the information they are given and the progression routes they take may depend on the incidental knowledge, preferences and skills of tutors or other 'key' people, which is why the volunteer or 'signposting' training courses initiated in some areas are of such potential importance. However, some guidance workers fear that wrong or misleading information may be offered by people who are not trained specialist guidance workers:

Though advice should be available it should be given by qualified and experienced staff. We can't expect teaching staff to become guidance workers just because it's the final session of a course. The move towards guidance being given by subject tutors is not realistic. Nor can we expect other people who aren't specialised to give information. I've found that people in job centres often give the wrong information, telling people they are ineligible or too old to do certain things.
(Outreach guidance worker)

Tutors do, however, have an extremely important role in learner progression, not least one of encouragement and support: *'Little [progression] can be achieved without the support of well-informed, trained and sympathetic staff'* (Munn Tett and Arney, 1993). They should, at the very least, be able to pass on to learners details of other learning opportunities relevant to their subject area as well as details of local guidance workers or services and other sources of help and support. Nevertheless, if a 'critical mass' of people are to move from an informal to a formal learning environment, they will need access or referrals to well-informed, locally-based guidance workers for whom adequate basic training should be provided:

There's nothing below NVQ2 – nothing to recognise the experience of people. There's a lack of foundation level accreditation for those working in a range of community contexts. There are some OCN Units but we need something more coherent'. (Outreach guidance worker)

Mobile guidance services
Many people have been helped back into learning as a result of mobile guidance services that offer educational information and advice in settings such as shopping centres and car parks, and act as brokers linking the community and the voluntary sector with education and training providers. Examples include the Liverbus, part of Liverpool Educational Guidance network and the LEA community education service; Dove Valley Community Bus in South Derbyshire based at Hatton Community school and funded by Derbyshire County Council Education Department, and the Bolton Opportunities Bus.

Bolton Opportunities Bus visits sites within socially deprived areas of Bolton. It operates three days a week as a children's playbus and another three as a mobile resource unit offering information, advice and education. The bus has been converted to provide IT training and has six computers, a tutorial room and a fully equipped, free crèche.

The initiative was the idea of access development officers at Bolton Institute of Higher Education. They manage the project and employ a co-ordinator/outreach worker and a bus driver. Funding has been provided from a variety of sources: HEFCE, the Single Regeneration Budget, Bolton City Challenge, Bolton Leisure Services and Bolton Community Education Service. Bolton Leisure Services provides play facilities, Bolton Community Education Service provides tutors and Bolton College provides advice and guidance workshops. All advice and education provision is free.

The project aims to help individuals back into education and training. All users have the opportunity to receive one-to-one educational guidance and the IT training is linked to a nationally recognised qualification. To help people take advantage of other local learning opportunities, the co-ordinator has found that she sometimes needs to accompany them to community education centres: 'We have learned that you cannot underestimate the barriers caused by lack of confidence and low self-esteem'.

Users of the bus include unemployed people, women returners, single parents, ethnic minority residents and other groups who do not have the confidence to approach education and training providers. (HEFCE, 1998)

A strategic approach to guidance

Two large national voluntary organisations that work widely in local communities – the WEA and the NFWI – have adopted a strategic approach to guidance in order to assist the educational progression of their members

The WEA has been conducting a project to develop a structured approach to educational guidance, the aim of which is to ensure that participants in all courses, even those which are informal and non-accredited, should have access to educational guidance at any stage that they may require it: pre-entry and at entry, on-course, and pre-exit. It is stressed that this guidance should be impartial and embedded in equal opportunities policy and practice, and that it should be informal, voluntary, flexible and responsive to students' needs.

To achieve these aims, work has been conducted on identifying minimum standards for the provision of guidance throughout the National Association. All Districts produced action plans for guidance in 1997-98 and the project has been supporting them in implementing, monitoring and evaluating these schemes. A Student Entitlement for all learners has been agreed and this now forms part of the revised WEA Charter. It states:

- That pre-course information should help individuals decide if the course is right for them and where appropriate, they should be referred to other educational providers or guidance providers.
- That, while on the course, students should have detailed information about it and of what is expected of them; should be offered help with planning their learning and given the opportunity to discuss their progress.
- That, before the end of the course, students should be given information regarding their achievements and what they could do next. Where required they would be referred to other providers of education or impartial guidance.

Guidelines for tutors on helping students to consider progression routes have been produced in the eastern District. (WEA, 1997a)

Between 1995 and 1998, the National Federation of Women's Institutes conducted a **Rural Guidance Project** funded by the Department of Education and Employment. The aims were to help members understand the role and nature of guidance, its potential for helping individuals and its role in relation to NFWI's own learning activities.

The DfEE grant was used to fund three weekend training workshops for WI representatives at Denman College. After attending the workshops, each participant was invited to carry out a project of her own choosing for which she received a £50 grant to defray costs.

The resulting projects varied widely: some were centred on one institute whilst others spanned a federation. Some members devised questionnaires which they circulated to members; others concentrated on building up networks with other providers of continuing education.

Following her participation in the workshops, the member from Warwickshire contacted local adult guidance providers and this resulted in members of her federation joining networks where the WI had not been represented before. She also set out to increase members' awareness of WI education opportunities and Open College Network accreditation. She produced explanatory leaflets which were sent to all WIs; had an information stand at various Federation meetings and went to speak to groups about OCNS. As a result of these activities, the number of OCN certificates awarded to WI members doubled.

Following the Guidance workshops, the Leicestershire representative produced two leaflets: one on where members might go for further guidance and education provision and another entitled *Learning Opportunities in the WI*. These were circulated throughout her Federation. The latter listed all the WI learning opportunities available and highlighted the role of NFWI's National Tutors. This generated a number of requests for courses, 10 of which have been delivered in response.

A booklet entitled *Routes to lifelong learning opportunities towards the 21st century from NFWI* has been produced with DfEE funding and is being distributed nationally.
(Source: Anne Stamper, education adviser to the NFWI)

Institution-based guidance

Within individual education institutions, the amount and quality of advice and guidance provided for incoming and continuing students varies considerably. Inadequate initial guidance can significantly hamper learner progress, especially that of people coming from a less formal learning environment. A study based on national and institutional research found that many learners who failed to complete programmes of study in further or higher education had received little or no pre-entry guidance (McGivney, 1996). The evidence collected for that study indicated that learners preparing to enter higher level programmes need, as well as straightforward information on the dates, times and locations of learning, explicit information and guidance on:

- The suitability of the programme to the individual's experience and goals.
- The entry qualifications or previous experience needed.
- The topics and subjects to be covered and the depth of coverage.
- The expected workload.
- The type and frequency of assessments.
- Recommended reading (pre-course and course texts).
- All direct and indirect costs.
- Potential sources of financial assistance.
- Potential post course employment and education routes.

- Information about alternative programmes and providers if the desired programme is not appropriate.

Guidance should not just be available when people are beginning an education programme. It is widely accepted that it should be provided throughout a learning pathway together with other necessary supports.

Support for transition

Outreach workers have found that inviting college staff to talk to informal learners or arranging group visits to institutions, helps to familiarise learners with a different educational environment and gives them the confidence to enrol in formal learning programmes. (Blackwell, 1997)

Sometimes community education and guidance workers accompany learners on their first session of a formal education programme in a college. Another common strategy is to invite more experienced adult learners to act as ambassadors and provide encouragement and tips for those about to start a formal learning programme.

Some practitioners have found an effective approach is to provide 'half and half' programmes where people start learning in the community then move on as a group to a more formal setting, with high levels of support.

In Scotland, some specially designed, community-based bridging courses have been established to enable students to progress from individual modules undertaken in the community to college courses. In Edinburgh, for example, Stevenson College has developed **Pathway and Headway** courses in partnership with Platform and the Wester Hailes Education Centres and these act as a bridge to college-based programmes. Such arrangements allow individuals to complete a programme of modules, including core skills, in the community before considering full-time education or training: *'This has made the leap from community-based to formal provision less challenging for many and has developed useful partnerships amongst providers'.* (Scottish Office, 1996)

Mentors

Some individuals, especially those from disadvantaged groups, require the continuing support of a 'key' person to assist their progression into employment or formal education or training. 'Buddy' or mentoring schemes based on a particular personal relationship, have helped a number of individuals settle into institutional-based programme.

Mentoring is a long-term guide counsellor and (sometimes) friend whose insights and view you come to value as you experience various transitions in your life and career. In some ways akin to the apprenticeships of the past, mentoring relationships have been reinstated today as a way of passing on the knowledge and experience of one person to another (Channel Four Television, 1995)

A community education project in Scotland organised a **'Chumming'** scheme whereby a tutor from community education was allocated to each student moving to further education to help them manage the transition. The tutor accompanied the student to the college and was a source of contact for college staff if any problems arose. (Munn, Tett and Arney, 1993)

At **Lewisham College**, more experienced learners act as 'study buddies' for people who are new to college learning. The initiative is part of the FEFC-funded initiative *Inclusive Learning* which aims to match individual learning needs to the learning environment.

Some mentoring schemes have been targeted specifically at the Black communities with the aim of helping them to make a successful transition into learning or employment: Manchester Metropolitan University and the universities of North and East London have such schemes, while Goldsmiths college runs a Black Teachers Mentoring Scheme for trainee teachers.

Supportive learning groups

A vital component in encouraging learning continuation and progression is group or peer support. Some of the practitioners consulted during this study considered this to be one of the most important factors in learner continuation and progression. People feel comfortable in a familiar group and often keep each other going by providing bonding, mutual encouragement and support:

> *Once people feel security as a group they start to move on. New things come into their lives and people with common interests. People use groups for as long as they need then go off into different things as their confidence grows.* (Outreach worker)

A college informant endorsed this view, confiding that open and distance learning approaches do not always provide the kind of group support that is necessary to encourage continuation:

> *The drop-out here from open learning and flexible workshops is horrendous. They go there and don't know anyone. We have independent learning routes with computer links but again retention is bad. When we have drop-in support they meet a 'group' and tend then to drop the independent learning and become part of the group.*

Providing these kinds of support for learners may be expensive but studies indicate that it can save costs in the longer term by leading to higher retention and achievement rates. (Munn, MacDonald and Lowden, 1992; McGivney, 1996). In one of the Park Lane College adult learning centres in Leeds, 70 per cent of GCSE passes were from former adult basic education students: *'because they had been adequately supported'*.

9 Obstacles to learner progression and the development of progression routes

The preceding sections have highlighted some of the ways in which learners can be encouraged and helped to move between different forms and levels of learning activity. Where there are people, structures and services in place to provide learning routes and support learner transition, rates of progression (in any direction) are often high. Where these are lacking, they are, not surprisingly, much lower. As stated in an earlier study (McGivney, 1992), progression data need to be put in context. If they are not accompanied by evidence on the extent and nature of learning routes, strategies to promote educational progression and support to sustain student progression, there is a danger that a low rate of progression may be interpreted as lack of interest or motivation on the part of adult learners. Sometimes, of course, it is due to their circumstances and wishes; at other times, however, it is the result of external factors including constraints on education providers. There is a clear distinction to be drawn between barriers that affect the learner and those that affect the provider.

Constraints on learners

The kind of problems that prevent individual learners from continuing on an educational pathway are well known. They include:

- Insufficient information and guidance on further learning opportunities.
- Lack of clear progression routes.
- Lack of staff encouragement.
- Reluctance to move from a familiar local environment.
- Negative perceptions of further and higher education institutions.
- Inability to meet costs.
- Lack of practical support mechanisms such as help with childcare, transport or physical access arrangements for people with disabilities.
- Inconvenient timing and location of learning programmes.
- Other commitments (employment, domestic responsibilities).
- Lack of support from family members.
- Transport problems. (McGivney, 1992 and 1994)

Practical problems such as costs and domestic commitments are the most commonly cited barriers to progression (and to participation in general). Research into the outcomes for people on OCN-accredited programmes (FEU, 1993) typically found that the learners who did not progress to other learning opportunities were prevented from doing so mainly by family commitments, inability to meet costs, lack of appropriate courses and employment-related reasons. Most subsequent studies of participation and progression issues suggest that these still represent considerable barriers for many adults.

Financial barriers

It is often not lack of motivation that prevents people from embarking on formal learning but lack of money.

During the recent evaluation of the Higher Education Funding Council funding programme for non award bearing continuing education (McNair, 1999), staff in some participating institutions expressed fears that few individuals in the groups they were working with would be able to continue learning if they had to pay for opportunities when HEFCE funding ended. This situation is frequently found by those providing community-base learning. It is not just course fees that create the problem: even if courses are free or low cost, there can be other costs relating to travel, childcare, books, equipment and examination fees. According to a college outreach worker, the registration fees charged by some examining bodies are 'horrendously expensive' for people on low incomes. It was pointed out that whereas there may be some financial support for people on welfare benefits, those who earn very low wages get little or no financial help with educational costs. As a result their ability to participate is significantly reduced: *'for many students participating in community-based learning even the smallest cost can prove a disincentive'.* (Scottish Office, 1996: 29). Career development loans are not a feasible option for such people. Ironically, it is the part of the educational spectrum that attracts most non traditional learners – informal, non-accredited, learning programmes – that receives the least financial support. The NIACE 1997-98 survey of fees charged to part-time adult students by local authorities and colleges, notes in relation to non-Schedule 2 provision that: *'the impact of cuts has come through to learners in steep fee increases and less generous or more tightly targeted concessions.'* (Winkless, 1999: 3)

The report of the Further Education Student Support Advisory Group on student support arrangements in further education (DfEE, 1998c) identified a number of concerns:

- Under current arrangements, the availability of financial support varies in different parts of the country – students in the same circumstances, with the same needs, are not entitled to receive the same support.
- Expenditure on discretionary awards for further education has been reducing dramatically. it has almost halved between 1992/93 to 1995/96 and is still falling.
- There is virtually no financial support for education available to students after age 18. Adults can study part-time while they are in receipt of the Jobseeker's Allowance but many have to stop part way through their course to take a job when one is offered.
- There is a lack of clarity and consistency about people's entitlement to state benefits when they are in education.

The report recommended that, for learners aged 19+ on low incomes, there should be national minimum entitlements for financial support to meet the costs of travel, childcare, fees and other costs of education. Learners on low incomes should be exempt from all tuition and examination fees as well as registration fees, and eligibility for college Access funds should be extended to part-time students.

Although there have been considerable improvements in financial support for adult learners since that report was published, including increases in college Access funds, extension of loans to part-time students on low incomes and those aged up to 55, and the waiving of fees for unemployed higher education students on benefits, some of the concerns noted above are still relevant.

Benefit rules

Benefit rules still constitute a considerable barrier to adults' ability to undertake sustained programmes of education or training. A study of the effects of the 16-hour study rule (Donnelly, 1997) typically found that unemployed people who wish to study are frequently prevented from doing so. This is partly attributed to the complexity of Benefit rules and regulations and the wide variations in the ways these are still interpreted and applied. The study revealed inconsistent operation of the rules by different benefit offices and staff members; different definitions of full-time and part-time courses, and disruption of learning programmes because of compulsory interviews and government programmes. Several colleges responding to the study commented on the incompatibility between people's desire to study and gain a qualification and the Employment Service's need to meet specified targets.

These problems affect not only unemployed individuals but also those trying to assist them. A worker involved in the Coalfields Learning Project referred to the negative effect of the *'benefits merry-go-round'* on attempts to implement learning programmes:

> *The Benefits Agency will only deal with individual cases therefore it's difficult to get a co-ordinated response to work with groups. It's difficult to design things for people on benefits because you don't know how it's going to affect them financially. Building in work experience is difficult under the 16-hour rule.*

Structural barriers

The absence of clear learning routes has an inevitable impact on rates of educational progression. Several studies have indicated that this is one of the principal obstacles to movement between different types and levels of learning. Previous NIACE research showed that the development of progression pathways was patchy and uneven across institutions and sectors. In some areas there were few links between formal education providers and grassroots or community education providers and insufficient attempts to articulate college outreach programmes with higher level mainstream programmes (McGivney, 1992 and 1994).

Lack of cross sectoral collaboration in developing learning pathways was also cited as an obstacle to progression in a Further Education Development Agency study (FEDA, 1995). This found that although there were partnerships between colleges, schools and universities which were facilitating linear learning pathways, there was relatively little partnership activity focusing on progression from adult education into college-based Schedule 2 provision. Where partnerships had developed between adult and further education providers, especially on a franchising basis, colleges were finding that they we able to recruit new client groups who had been first attracted by a non vocational curriculum offer.

A Scottish study of community-based learning also revealed a paucity of links enabling cross sectoral collaboration and planning:

> *Although impressive progress has been made in offering a range of provision at local level, careful planning of progression routes for adults has been less evident. While this has been due, in part, to funding restrictions, it has also reflected a lack of cross-sectoral programme planning and, in some cases, an ad hoc approach to delivery.* (Scottish Office, 1996: 30)

The situation inevitably varies across geographical areas. Community-based education and development workers contacted during the current study reported excellent reciprocal relationships with some colleges and other sector providers, but little contact with others, and this obviously restricted the extent of progression options they could bring to the notice of learners. In one area some colleges were allegedly reluctant to incur the expenditure required to develop the kind of arrangements that facilitate the participation and progression of non-traditional learners: *'They lack interest in collaborating with voluntary organisations to create learning pathways and are unresponsive to local learning needs'*. In another area, it was reported that local colleges were ostensibly engaged in developing pathways but did not deliver the goods when learning needs were identified: *'There's a problem of raising expectations that are not met: broken promises from providers. We can motivate people in the community but providers sometimes let us down.'*

Many people hoped that the development of lifelong learning partnerships would help to create better cross-sectoral working relationships although some feared that these might turn into something too large and bureaucratic to assist grassroots learning initiatives.

Psychological and social barriers

The practical barriers to educational progression are frequently compounded by others. For some groups and individuals, engaging in formal education involves not only economic but also social and psychological costs. Many suffer from lack of confidence, perceptions of being too old to attend an education institution or anxieties about leaving familiar territory and 'comfort zones'. Some segments of the population, male manual workers for example, fear that participation in formal education may reflect badly on them and result in loss of status (McGivney, 1999). Many men see their role as worker not learner and feel that a return to learning might be interpreted as failure. As one of the Coalfields development workers explained: *'[They've had] centuries of not needing qualifications in order to go down the pit. Times have changed but attitudes haven't'*.

Perceptions

Outdated perceptions of the formal education sector are another obstacle to progression. Colleges are still widely seen as exclusively for younger learners and higher education institutions for a professional elite. A number of studies (McGivney, 1990, 1992, 1994) have found that many people automatically assume that the programmes provided in further and higher education are beyond their financial and intellectual reach and that qualifications are always required as a condition for entry.

Suspicion of formal education providers

Some groups have traditionally been neglected by formal education providers and regard current attempts to attract them with some cynicism. According to one informant, this applies particularly to older learners:

> *Up to about two or three years ago, everything was happening in the voluntary sector and nothing in the formal education world. It had no interest or was so perceived and the links were not there. I would think that may still be partially true though efforts have been made to bridge that gap and overcome the distrust. But whenever FE has attempted to do this they have been greeted with great suspicion as only looking for 'bums on seats'.*

Difficulties in adjusting to formal education

Those who do make the transition from informal community-based learning to a formal learning environment sometimes experience difficulty in adjusting to the differences in ethos and ways of working. Some people working with informal learners claimed that staff in colleges and other institutions do not always appreciate the gap between community-based and institutional learning, even if the latter is ostensibly not very formal. The problems are manifold and not just related to the style and content of learning programmes. Guidance workers have found that even enrolment forms can be a deterrent to new learners and many are also intimidated by the language used in college literature and procedures. Some have also been put off by not having a friendly or helpful reception on their first solo visit to a learning institution. A community education worker on a large estate reported that an unsatisfactory first contact with an educational institution deters not only individuals but also their networks of family, friends and acquaintances: *'if it is not a good experience the word spreads immediately'*.

Constraints on providers

Policy issues

Some of the changes in education and funding policies in recent years have had a detrimental effect on progression routes from informal learning. According to one informant, incorporation of colleges after the 1992 Further and Higher Education Act led to the loss of vital community links which are now having to be reforged:

> *Colleges used to have closer links with community pre incorporation. The money has been drained out of the community education service. Some LEAs handed all community education over to colleges. Sometimes this resulted in the loss of a lot of the networks that had been built up. Providers are now having to recreate and rework network models.*

Another consequence of the Act has been loss of support for informal, community-based learning. Finding finance for unaccredited, informal learning was a problem repeatedly cited by community providers:

> *People in the community are coming together in groups to help themselves but they can't access any support. The needs are there and well demonstrated but funding streams to meet their needs are lacking.*

> *Our biggest problem is that no-one wants to pay for informal learning. They want to pay for accreditation of A, B or C. The development part needs a lick of paint.*

> *Formal learning in areas like this won't get off the ground until we recognise the connection between community development, informal learning and formal learning.*

> *Our informal non-Schedule 2 work is only pump-primed.*

One place visited during the course of the study, Langold Community Resources Centre (see pp 14-16), illustrated the problem. Although a vital community resource which was contributing to capacity-building and local regeneration as well as acting as a gateway to learning for many people, the centre was, at the time of the visit, experiencing difficulty securing continuing funding to meet needs. In some ways it was a victim of its own success: as the numbers of people using the centre increased, it was becoming increasingly difficult to respond to needs on an unpaid volunteer basis.

European funding

Some of the local groups and organisations contacted had only been able to provide education and training activities with the help of European funding:

> *It's European funding that's enabling these things to happen. We kick start the movement upwards.*

Trails are being blazed thanks to Objectives 1 and 2: without these we would not have been able to do anything.

However, some providers of informal education were experiencing increasing difficulty in obtaining the necessary matched funding: *'Everything we do is totally fragile and precarious. Doors are closing all round. There are crevices of European funding but not enough to match it.'*

One of the problems identified was that some organisations cannot promise matched funding because they do not know in advance whether they will be able to make good their pledge.

Colleges also reported problems in relation to European funding. A lecturer explained that although some European funding programmes such as Objective 2 are underspent, they cannot be drawn down because of lack of matched finding and strings attached. He complained that in certain circumstances, the FEFC claws back funding when a college obtains European money:

It's only beneficial for a college to have ESF if it isn't hitting or exceeding its targets. If you get ESF for training, the FEFC will only give you 55 per cent of the units and says it will use the 45 per cent in other areas. However, as most European programmes are targeted regionally or locally this argument does not stand up. It also says that if it doesn't claw back there will be double funding. This contradicts the principle of additionality. There are loads of things that the FEFC won't fund and you can only use ESF on what the FEFC will allow you to do. If you complain to the EC they say it's the individual FEC that is not playing fair and the college then suffers not the FEFC.

FEFC funding

Many of the people who reported to this project considered FEFC funding too inflexible to help people who are non-traditional learners. Those who were developing FEFC-funded progression routes felt they had lost the flexibility and student-centred ethos of earlier informal learning as a result of requirements to do with student numbers and pre determined outcomes, both of which can be difficult to achieve with some groups of adult learners. As one education development worker argued:

The relating of funding and quality measures doesn't work with non traditional learning and can risk loss of creativity, experiment and innovation. Quality measures applied in the statutory sector may be difficult to apply to informal learning. The Standards Fund has a quality system in it that will work across the AE service but it will be difficult to apply in an informal community education. This doesn't mean that quality shouldn't be safeguarded.

Several people working informally in the community commented that linking funding to progression outcomes is not always appropriate as the results of learning are not always immediate or visible. According to an outreach guidance worker:

For many people, learning progression is gradual and there may be a time lag between informal learning and any next stage. You need to give people time. They're not necessarily going to move straight on to the next step.

Inappropriate qualifications

Some of the community-based providers contacted felt there were pressures on them to use qualifications they considered inappropriate for the groups they were working with. A college outreach worker developing progression routes in a rural area had experienced pressure from a

Training and Enterprise Council to put new learners through NVQs: *'Sometimes something like an RSA is better but TECs consider NVQs are the most important type of certification. Sometimes NVQs are a handicap to progression'*. To illustrate this, she cited the example of nursing students who had entered higher education with an NVQ3 but found they had no underpinning scientific knowledge and were therefore at a disadvantage compared to those entering with A Levels or Access qualifications: *'This leads to drop-out'*.

Unequal partnerships

The development of learning pathways can be disrupted by lack of genuine partnership. Smaller organisations are sometimes at a disadvantage in relation to larger and better resourced partners. In one instance reported, a tenants' group that had been involved in a local funding application was excluded from decision-making by the local council once funding was approved. In another instance, a college that was running classes for parents in a local primary school did not communicate adequately with the school and remained largely aloof from it. There was also perceived to be an element of exploitation: the school was doing all the recruitment and providing stationery and learning materials while the college only supplied tutors. As a result, some schools did not wish to work with the college again.

Reluctance to refer students to other provision

Several of the community-based workers contacted had found that some organisations and institutions try and keep people with them rather than referring them to other learning providers. This tendency has also been identified in studies of adult learning routes. One conducted in Scotland noted that some providers encouraged 'sideways' rather than 'upwards and outwards' moves. This was particularly the case with community-based organisations providing non formal education where there was not a subject-centred culture:

> *In the past, their orientation has often been to sustaining participation within their systems rather than moving students onwards and upwards. Providers and participants alike may have suffered from a fear of letting go of the supportive situation which they were providing or participating in.*
> (Munn, Tett and Arney, 1993: 18)

Reluctance to refer people on can be for purely financial reasons: *'It can be a financial disadvantage if individuals move on and they want to hang on to their numbers to get funding'* (Community education worker). Sometimes, however, it is because community-based groups and organisations have developed a strong group ethos and sense of solidarity which can lead to over-protectiveness and a parochial, inward-looking attitude. This inevitably limits progression to other learning environments:

> *Because of the way they have developed and their strong local community ethos, there is a danger that local centres have ghettoised provision. They need to build links so that people can progress outside the immediate locality. It is important that neighbourhood centres and colleges be encouraged to look outside themselves.* (Adult education organiser in a rural area)

Lack of policies on progression and student tracking

Some institutions have explicit policies on progression and have developed visible learning pathways for students to follow. Others have no such policy and, as found in a Scottish study, strategies to encourage educational progression tend to be intermittent and *ad hoc* (Munn, Tett and Arney, 1993). The same study found that some practitioners were sceptical about the value of having a progression policy: *'fearing that it might become a straitjacket and narrow the range of opportunities for students'*. However, the mere fact of having a policy can motivate reflection on different ways of developing and facilitating learning pathways. To ensure that it is effective, such a policy would need to be backed up by good monitoring procedures. Some providers do not yet routinely collect and record information about earlier informal learning pathways, progression from informal learning to mainstream or progression from non-Schedule 2 to Schedule 2 provision.

The new lifelong learning partnerships offer a good opportunity to develop procedures for inter-institutional, intra institutional and cross sectoral student tracking. The good practice that already goes on in some areas needs to be shared

A pilot **Passport to Learning** scheme started in Nottinghamshire in September 1998. The aim is to monitor and track the progression of participants in community learning programmes supported by Nottinghamshire County Council. The scheme provides an individual planning profile for adult students and is a means of tracking links between different elements of provision. It is linked to a database which allows for more effective reporting for SRB funding purposes. (Source: *Fast Forward*)

None of the obstacles to progression mentioned above are insurmountable. As the earlier case studies demonstrate, many people take a variety of progression routes from informal community-based learning *when there are well judged interventions, structures and arrangements that encourage and enable them to do so.*

10 Concluding observations

Although informal learning is the most widespread form of learning, until very recently it has received relatively little recognition and investment. This could be partly due to its sheer diversity. Informal learning is difficult to pin down in an exact definition: it can be unpremeditated, self-directed, intentional and planned. It can be generated by individuals; it can be a collective process arising from grassroots concerns or social protest); it can be initiated by outside agencies responding to community interests or education providers who wish to offer previously excluded groups learning opportunities in their own environment.

Informal learning takes place in a huge variety of settings. These may include dedicated learning environments such as community education centres and schools, but are more likely to be non-educational settings such as village halls, community centres, clubs, voluntary groups, shopping centres or pubs. Voluntary organisations and community groups are significant providers of informal learning. The importance of the local setting should not be under-estimated. People working with groups in the community find that the location of learning is extremely important, often more so than its actual focus. This is due not only to practical but to psychological and cultural factors. In some areas it is found that people are very reluctant to go outside their familiar local boundaries: *'In inner-city areas only very local centres can help make education accessible to individuals and communities otherwise excluded by distance, transport or cultural barriers'* (Fryer, 1997).

During the course of the study visits were made to various settings in which informal learning was taking place. These included:

- Outreach locations used by formal institutions.
- A 'shop and learn' complex.
- A regional scheme for community development and regeneration.
- A resource and leisure centre.
- A community centre involved in providing community support, advice and education.
- An adult residential college.
- Two junior schools.

Learning outcomes

Such a small number of examples clearly cannot do justice to the immense variety of informal learning locations and arrangements. They can, however, give an idea of some of the processes involved in informal learning and its outcomes.

Community-based informal learning plays a critical role in widening participation in excluded communities – people who are educationally, economically and socially disadvantaged. The people who had been attracted to the informal learning provision profiled in the study were people in low income groups, long-term unemployed people, people with no qualifications, people suffering from multiple deprivation (the homeless, etc.).

An important point to make is that informal learning is often, initially, unconnected with education. It is impossible to quantify the amount of informal learning that is undertaken in the community not only because of its scale and diversity but because it is often both a part and a product of ostensibly non educational activities. For the same reason it is difficult to measure its overall impact. Nevertheless there is substantial evidence that, whether planned or unpremeditated, informal learning can lead to a number of important and mutually reinforcing benefits for learners. In all of the instances reported in previous sections, community-based learning had led to significant self-development outcomes such as:

- Development of knowledge and understanding and, often, new practical skills.
- Improved personal and social skills (such as better communication skills, parenting skills).
- Significantly increased self-confidence and self-esteem.
- Greater autonomy.

It had also motivated and helped many people to progress in one or several of the following ways:

- Changes in life style, quality of life or personal life.
- Involvement in further learning in different places and at different levels.
- Wider involvement in the local community (more active citizenship).
- Movement into employment, self-employment or voluntary work.

The proportions of people taking these routes inevitably varied widely in different informal learning situations. In many cases, as reported in the *Drome* survey (Maxwell, 1997), individuals take more than one progression route, and this was confirmed by the examples used during this study. However, the examples also suggested that different models of informal learning produce slightly different patterns of progression. Informal learning generated by local people themselves most often leads to wider community involvement and activism. The learning arranged by education providers most often leads to high rates of educational progression (as they have the necessary links and information on progression options). Informal and incidental learning of the kind gained in voluntary organisations most often leads to job acquisition, changes of career and wider involvement in the community. Most importantly, informal learning initiatives linked with community development and regeneration such as the Coalfields Partnerships offer deprived individuals and communities a route out of despair and depression.

Informal learning can result in important benefits not only for the individual but for the family, the community or society as a whole. Many of the examples of informal learning seen in the course of this study were having an important 'ripple' or multiplier effect. Social networks in some excluded communities are very strong. As one community education has experienced, you may have a regular learning group of 15 but *'an active periphery of 80'* as people pass on the benefits of their learning to the wider community:

It's not just the group that are ostensibly involved. It operates by a cascade process. Information is passed on and cascades out into the community. There are organic networks and if informal learning can tap into these you can achieve far more than with those you meet on a regular basis. You can have a major impact in terms of social stability with a piece of learning that involves eight people. The key is to use kinship or wider family networks, and train people to disseminate information in forms that are easily replicable.

A college outreach tutor working in a deprived area in Leeds typically found that: *'people want to involve their families – bring their mums'*. Other contacts had found that when parents are learning, their children are motivated to do likewise: *'there's an effect on the next generation'*. Informal learners reported that their enjoyment and achievements had stimulated their family and friends to follow their example. This again confirms previous research findings. A study of learning in local voluntary organisations revealed: *'strong evidence of transmission of individual learning to close family and friends'* and *'a windfall of human capital that society has not yet fully recognised or invested in productively. The result is a rapid and all too often ignored and wasted development of human potential'* (Elsdon, 1995: 48).

The role of informal education in widening participation and encouraging progression

The field visits confirmed previous research findings in showing that community-based informal learning plays a critical role in widening participation in excluded communities. It also sets many people on a continuing learning path by helping them to become confident and successful learners. In the words of one practitioner: *'it uncovers myriad possibilities'*. Many of the individuals who engage in informal learning do not have educational progression as a primary (or even secondary) aim. Many would not even identify themselves as learners. In most of the cases outlined in previous chapters, 'onward and upward' progression to structured formal learning was unplanned and unanticipated. Very few of the people involved would have considered entering formal education programmes without prior engagement in informal learning. It was the positive learning experience in a familiar local environment that had stimulated new interests and enthusiasms and motivated people to continue learning. Two informal learners interviewed during the course of the study described the momentum that builds up as a result of engaging in informal learning:

'Once you've made the move it's like being on a bus: you want to keep moving'.

'There's a snowball effect: your confidence builds and you want to do more.'

The study indicated that involvement in informal learning often follows a similar pattern despite the huge diversity of learning arrangements, activities and settings. People start learning informally for a variety of reasons often arising out of their immediate interests, priorities and concerns. Since much informal learning is embedded in non educational activities and does not take the form of a taught course, it is not always recognised as learning. During it, however, confidence grows and aspirations and expectations are aroused. New interests and needs are identified and at this point learning often becomes conscious and explicit. According to one community outreach worker: *'People see what they are doing as relevant to their interests not education in the abstract. They suddenly see that education can be relevant. This is a huge leap'*. At this stage learners are often ready to move on to more structured, learning activities. In order to do so, however, they need information, encouragement, coherent progression routes and support structures.

Factors that facilitate progression

The evidence indicates that the factors that enable people to continue learning are:

1 The intervention and help of 'key' individuals who inform, motivate, enthuse, encourage and advise individuals and groups and act as intermediaries between them and education providers. These are not always education or guidance workers but can be health visitors, community workers, volunteers, pre-school playgroup leaders etc.

2 Structures and services that enable progression (information and guidance services; inter-agency partnerships, Open College Networks, access networks, links between informal and formal providers).

3 Flexible and responsive education/training providers and systems.

4 Provision of informal and formal learning opportunities at the same site.

5 Provision that responds to identified interests and needs and encourages progression by including confidence-building activities, planning for progression and processes to recognise achievements (e.g. portfolios, accreditation).

6 Programmes designed to help people learn incrementally (accredited programmes; Access courses, bridging courses, Return to Learn, etc.)

7 Strategies that enable progression between different learning levels (modular approaches, accreditation frameworks, APEL; articulation between outreach and mainstream provision).

8 Support mechanisms that help people overcome any obstacles that might have prevented them from engaging in formal learning (help with finance, travel, childcare; provision of learning support such as basic education, help with English language; study skills).

The first of these – key people – emerged as the most important factor in encouraging people to continue learning and to progress from informal to formal programmes. Without the support of local outreach and guidance workers or other people working in the community, many individuals would not make the transition to formal education or training programmes.

The *obstacles* to learner progression are well known – lack of encouragement, information and guidance; insufficient networking and links between sectors and providers; absence of appropriate next learning steps and bridging programmes; insufficient mechanisms and arrangements facilitating movement between different learning environments and levels; lack of practical help and support for learners. In addition to these, the evidence from this study suggests that there is sometimes little appreciation of how big a gap there is for many people between informal and formal learning. Many learners need preparatory or intermediate courses before they are ready to move into a more formal education or training programme, especially one that is provided in an educational institution.

It should be stressed, however, that progression within education or training is only one outcome of informal learning, albeit an important and desirable one. Many adults who engage in informal learning do not wish to move into higher level education but have other learning goals:

Students who return to education because it enables them to play a fuller role in the community are involved as much in progression as students who are thinking mainly in terms of more courses or employment. None of these options are mutually exclusive and for the majority of students who come back into education it is likely that their ideas about what they might go on to are still tentative and in the process of forming, rather than completely fixed. It is therefore important to allow adult returners to define for themselves what progression means, rather than imposing some perhaps rather simplistic definition on all returners, regardless.
(Cordon, 1993: 25)

Sometimes a successful result for students will take them right off the map of educational progression into practical outcomes such as gaining employment or achieving a fuller membership of their community.
(Adkins, 1997: 135)

Supporting informal learning

Despite the importance of positive first learning experiences to lifelong learning and community development, informal learning activities are generally under-resourced. In the last decade, investment in community-based learning provided by Local Education Authorities and voluntary organisations has declined significantly. The greatest priority has been placed on programmes leading to qualifications and employment and those that ostensibly prepare people for higher levels of study. Other learning goals have received little or no attention. Many people involved in informal learning in the community consequently feel that their work is not sufficiently recognised and supported. During the course of the study informants repeatedly referred to the paucity of resources available for essential networking and development work:

> *Until we get local authorities and FE to take informal learning seriously we'll just be a bump on a log and the bit that always gets cut back.*

> *Our biggest problem is that no-one wants to pay for informal learning. They want to pay for accreditation of A, B or C. The development part needs a lick of paint.*

> *Formal learning in areas like this won't get off the ground until we recognise the connection between community development, informal learning and formal learning.*

> *Our informal non-Schedule 2 work is only pump-primed.*

> *Everything we do is totally fragile and precarious. Doors are closing all round. There are crevices of European funding but not enough to match it.*

Although they recognise that development work is time-consuming and labour-intensive, with uncertain outcomes in the short-term, community development workers believe that the long-term results justify greater investment.

Since the publication of *The Learning Age*, various sources of public funding have been introduced that will benefit the non formal sector. The Adult and Community Learning Fund, the new Standards Fund, Project 99 and the extension of the New Opportunities Fund will go some way towards supporting learning that leads to community development and capacity-building. In addition, the FEFC now has the power to support non-Schedule 2 provision and some pilot projects are being set up for disadvantaged groups. Although this development has been welcomed, many are worried by the stress in a recent FEFC Circular on the need for the pilots to be designed to lead to Schedule 2 provision. Informants to this study warned against imposing a progression and accreditation straitjacket on non-Schedule 2 work. Some fear that there is an official perception of informal learning as a *'sales spin'* or *'shop front'* to prepare people for the *'real stuff'*. They stressed that first-step learning should be valued for itself rather than as a route to more formal learning, qualifications and employment: *'Community-based learning should not be planned with the sole aim of pushing students up an educational ladder'*.

This is not a new debate, of course. Similar anxieties about informal learning being valued only as an instrument for other learning have been increasingly expressed during the last few years:

> *Each course is, or should be, complete in itself. To treat a course as no more than a ladder to the next course can have the effect of belittling the experience. As one tutor said, 'It is like saying that Monday is just a way of getting to Tuesday.'* (Adkins, 1997: 135)

We should ensure that education for the development of character, intellectual capacities and self-help in the voluntary sector continues to prosper and develop, not merely on order to secure important routes for employment or access to further learning, but equally, in the Aristotelian tradition, to promote civic and social responsibility and knowledge. As well as preparation for employment and access to vocational education, we should protect and develop democratic adult education in our communities so that they may develop knowledge and capacities. (Gurnah, 1997: 15)

The emphasis on vertical educational progression as the main outcome of first-step learning and pre-determined standards such as those applied in qualification courses are incompatible with the nature of informal learning which is essentially flexible and responsive to a diversity of groups and cultural values. It also takes insufficient account of adult learning patterns. With some disadvantaged groups such as the homeless, regular commitment to a learning programme is unlikely and learning groups are volatile: *'people drop out and new people drop in. We couldn't say you've got to come for the whole time: that would be another barrier'*. There is also considerable evidence that adult learning pathways are not always in a single direction. As research has confirmed, adults (and particularly women) develop more of a 'zig-zag' than a linear educational trajectory over their lifetime (Harre Hindemarsh and Davies, 1995). This is not necessarily a bad thing. One study (Munn, Tett and Arney, 1993) stresses the importance of enabling sideways as well as upward and outward progression on the grounds that continuing learning in the same setting or staying at the same learning level can help to develop learner confidence. In this country it has been found that even people involved in accredited programmes: *'flit across subject areas and levels'* (NOCN representative).

Moreover, for some disadvantaged groups and localities, it would be unrealistic to expect immediate outcomes in the form of movement to progressively more advanced levels of learning. People frequently pointed out during the course of this study that it can take a long time to raise the confidence and aspirations of people in the most disadvantaged geographical areas:

You're only scratching the surface in three years in trying to change these communities.

People here are hugely lacking in confidence. They often have no hope of being or doing anything.

The circumstances of some adults also inhibit immediate progression. Women with several children may be involved with community organisations, schools, playgroups or family centres over a number of years. Although informal learning activities in these environments may have a determining influence on their thinking and aspirations, many may be unable to undertake a formal education or training programme until their children are less dependent.

Many adults (. . .) require to spread their study over a number of years sometimes with long gaps between courses. They need integrated options which optimise individual attainment and ensure progression in line with the needs and aspirations of the learner. (Scottish Office, 1996: 8-9)

For many people too, the transition from informal to formal learning is a gradual process and some warn that it can be dangerous to refer individuals on too early:

There must be pathways and mechanisms in place to continue the momentum for adults to move on when they are ready. We should provide a variety of appropriate next steps to answer different needs. At the right point, motivation is assisted by the possibility of accreditation but if this is introduced too soon this can create too much pressure. (Local authority education worker)

Although it is important to provide incremental learning opportunities for all who want them, too strong an emphasis on linear progression may also undermine moves towards widening participation by stifling the flexibility and creativity of community-based learning. Coffield (1998: 5) argues that the current interest in informal learning: *'runs counter to the national moves to accredit learning formally and to increase the number and level of qualifications held by the workforce'*. As a practitioner working in a rural area commented:

> *The emphasis on progression and the types of evidence we are required to produce are leading to a narrowing of the diversity of provision at the first stage of return to learning. Provision now largely has to be marketed and developed with a very firm focus only on preparation for educational progression. This makes it difficult to attract and work with students who have traditionally been excluded, and who until they have a positive experience of participation, are unlikely to see any value in participating in a course that prepares them for progression in the educational system.*

Quality issues

Although important and desirable, qualifications are not the only measure of 'quality' in learning. However to state this raises several questions: what *is* quality in informal learning; which forms of informal learning should legitimately be supported and what criteria should be applied for funding informal learning?

In trying to define quality one might make a distinction between the nature and character of the learning (its content, general objectives and the way it is set up, organised and delivered); the support structures provided for learners; the achievements and results of the learning process for those involved; and the kind of 'exit' or continuation strategies to help learners progress.

Characteristics

The informal learning activities visited and used as examples during the course of this study had a number of features in common. They were all:

- Targeted at specific groups especially those who are disadvantaged socially, economically and educationally.
- Offered in informal community venues.
- Offered at low cost or free of charge.
- Provided in response to consultation with learners.
- Tailored to group or individual needs.
- Flexible in terms of delivery and content therefore could be adapted to emerging interests and circumstances of learners.
- Offered with a range of support services that help to eliminate barriers to participation in learning.

These features make learning accessible to people who traditionally have not participated in post school education or training and those with few qualifications. They should all therefore be considered as important indicators of quality.

A particularly strong feature of the examples of informal learning profiled in this report is that they allowed people to set their own learning agendas:

> *Well conceived educational strategies (...) which aim to make the disadvantaged authors of their own learning are the most promising strategies. They can 'reclaim' significant numbers of*

individuals and none of us can know what the effect may be when dormant potential is realised and released. (City of Coventry, undated: 21)

This is an essential mark of quality in informal learning. Research has shown that disadvantaged groups in the community do not embark on learning pathways as a result of exercising choice over what is already on offer but as a result of organisations responding to identified interests, negotiating options and customising provision (McIntyre and Kimberley, 1998). The case studies used in this study indicate that provision that is customised to the interests and requirements of new learners can have a greater and more positive impact on individuals and communities than the achievement of pre-determined objectives set by providers or examining bodies. A discussion group on child development run at a mother and toddlers' group is as valuable a learning activity as an accredited education or training course, and may have far more wide-reaching benefits.

Objectives and outcomes
Quality would also apply to the objectives of the learning. Informal learning is often a collective rather than an individual process, with people coming together as a group and seeking ways of responding to local issues and problems. This is a major difference between formal and informal education, and it is often not until people move on to more structured formal and accredited learning that it becomes a more individualised process. Learning that is entered into for the collective or community good should be considered as an important indicator of quality. (A type of community learning scheme that could usefully be extended throughout the country is one which trains local volunteers to act as 'learning champions', 'signposters' or 'brokers' for people in their own communities).

This study suggests that the kinds of informal learning that might be further supported are not those which are incidental, arising out of specific activities, but those which are entered into intentionally with the objective of bringing about a desired change either for the individual, a family or for the community. Change can be something tangible, such as acquiring new skills and competences or something subjective such as greater awareness and understanding. This reflects Eraut's (1997: 56) view that:

the use of the word 'learning' in 'the learning society' should refer only to significant changes in capability or understanding and exclude acquisition of further information which does not contribute to such changes. One advantage of this definition is that it can be applied at the group, organisational or societal levels as well as that of the individual.

To identify such changes, learners, both as individuals and as a group, should be encouraged, with the help of experienced adult education practitioners, to define the objectives of their learning (an action plan); to reflect on their learning at certain stages and to identify desired and other outcomes and the impact of these on the individual, the immediate family or the wider community. This would make it possible to measure the extent to which informal learning meets the objectives of participants; to identify the overall range of outcomes (which are invariably much wider than original learning objectives), and, together with post learning tracking, identify the progression routes subsequently taken. Some providers already conduct this kind of evaluation as part of their quality procedures.

Progression outcomes should not be too narrowly defined. To repeat what was said in Chapter 1, what may be a small step for one person may be a huge distance to travel for another. For a well educated person, the achievement of a new qualification could be the main progression outcome; for a young ex offender with literacy problems, a long-term unemployed person or an isolated lone parent, progression may be an apparently smaller but even more important achievement: having the confidence to express an opinion in a group; a perception of new opportunities and possibilities; the realisation that one has greater skills and capabilities than was previously thought. These are incremental outcomes, resulting from increased confidence, and they are legitimate and recordable signs of progression.

Maintaining the character of informal learning

The evidence collected for this study suggests that informal learning should receive recognition and support for its own sake and not be 'bureaucratised 'and transformed into something significantly different by funding regimes:

> *The cutting edge of radical adult education will almost inevitably be in the non formal community sector. Change, especially change to vision, social direction and community values can be assisted by legislation and good employment practices but relies more on non formal arrangements and informal learning in the community and the media, usually not identified separately as adult education at all.* (Duke, 1995: 256)

Hamilton (1996: 163) believes that Adult Basic Education has lost some of its innovative and dynamic quality, despite the successes of the last 10 years, as a result of being incorporated into the formal education system and certification processes. This is not a new phenomenon. In 1979, Fordham warned of the tendency for informal education to become more formal as a result of funding systems tied to particular outcomes and approaches. To argue against this tendency is not to suggest that pathways to structured formal and accredited education should not be developed for those who require and are ready for them. But if informal starting points were themselves transformed into something more formal and subjected to a range of constraints related to targets, many potential learners would be deterred. This would be counter productive. It is precisely the flexibility, creativity and responsiveness of much informal learning that opens up to people the possibility of engaging in formal and accredited learning.

People in the community need to learn what is relevant and important to them. The range and diversity of informal learning should not be stifled by funding regimes. It should be a cause of pride and celebration.

Points for policy makers arising from the study

To promote lifelong learning and avoid the continuation of a situation where we just have *'isolated islands of good practice'*, the following points should be taken into consideration by policy-makers and funding bodies.

- Greater value and status should be attached to informal learning as it can be a significant trigger for community development and regeneration as well as helping people to become confident learners.
- Lifelong learning policies should place particular emphasis on informal learning in community settings for, without prior participation in informal learning that is relevant to their interests and needs, many individuals would not have the confidence, the enthusiasm or the information to move to formal learning. Commitment of some public resources to the first learning experience is therefore a key to widening participation.
- First learning experiences should be valued for themselves as well as for their role in setting people on a learning pathway. Non-Schedule 2 provision should not be viewed only as a route to schedule-2 programmes.
- Funding methodologies that require pre-determined standards and outcomes are incompatible with flexible informal learning that is designed to respond to the requirements and interests of learners.
- It is important to recognise and support the diversity of progression routes from informal community-based learning. There is valuable learning that does not lead to qualifications or jobs: *'Concern with recognisable outcomes must enable people to define the outcomes which are important to them as citizens not just to the changes they can make to their chances in the labour market.'* (Jackson, 1995: 200)
- No specific subject area has a monopoly on encouraging educational progression. A significant finding of one research study (Maxwell, 1997) was that students were more likely to progress to education and training *when there was a liberal element to their programme* (my emphasis). Students who participated in programmes with a liberal element were more likely than average to progress along all (educational, vocational and community) progression routes.

Accreditation
- All learners have a right to have their learning achievements formally valued and recognised. For *those who want it* there should be opportunities to have their learning accredited.
- Inexperienced learners need more immediate benefits than long courses with a single qualification awarded at the end can provide. Credit-based programmes are particularly helpful to people with no or few qualifications and little experience of post-school education. A national, unit-based credit framework would help learner progression in two ways: smaller achievements would be recognised, which aids motivation, and credits could

be transferred across different institutions and providing agencies, which particularly helps adults whose ability to learn in one place may be constrained by employment or domestic circumstances.

- Open College Network accreditation provides a gradual and non threatening introduction to assessment and accreditation procedures. Open College Network accredited routes are extremely popular with learners in the community and deserve wider recognition and greater parity of esteem with other qualification frameworks.

- There are some areas that require consideration if a national credit framework is to be introduced:
  - Providers may need guidance on transferring credits between informal learning and learning in other environments.
  - There will need to be common approaches to entry requirements for different programmes of study.
  - Credit frameworks will need to be linked to, and give credit values to, existing qualifications.
  - More sophisticated record systems will be required, enabling tracking of achievements across different institutions, sectors and subject areas.

- Mechanisms for recognising and accrediting prior learning need to be further developed. Accreditation systems which enable linkages between informal learning, experiential learning and formal learning can significantly assist learner progression.

- It should be recognised that not all learners want or need accreditation. For some individuals any kind or level of accreditation may be a formidable barrier to participation. It is important therefore to support initiatives and programmes that have developed other means of identifying learning outcomes such as increased confidence and enhanced personal skills.

Funding issues

- Qualifications are not the only proxy for quality. This does not mean that non-accredited learning programmes should not be subject to quality standards but that they should not be driven largely by constraints to do with qualifications. There needs to be a way of funding learning routes for non traditional learners that is not tied to qualification outcomes

- Funding for community learning should not always be short term. Short-term funding leads to insecurity and vulnerability for many good initiatives and raises expectations that may be subsequently dashed. Consistent funding is more likely to bring about long- term change than short-term development funds

- Funding for informal learning needs to be flexible to meet the diversity of local needs, to allow for experiment and innovation and to enable programmes to start with small numbers. A funding system driven by numbers does not necessarily widen participation. In an informal learning context, the number of actual participants can be a misleading guide to the outcomes and impact of learning.

- Although informal learning may ostensibly only affect a few people, the potential *long-term* spin-offs are incalculable. There can be an impact on the family (their expectations and aspirations); on children (their school performance and perception of the value of education) and a significant growth in community activism.

- Funding systems need to allow realistic time-scales for the necessary development work to take place before outputs are required. It is unrealistic to expect rapid results in the most deprived areas. Many people have considerable barriers to overcome before they are ready to embark on a continuous learning path. Change can be a long-term process and some time may elapse before the outcomes of informal learning may be visible.

- The Adult and Community Learning Fund and New Opportunities Fund have a potentially critical role in helping community groups to provide learning opportunities. As neither is able to support all worthwhile initiatives, they could be strategically targeted at those groups and organisations that aim to provide learning that assists capacity building and community regeneration as well as offering opportunities for individual progression.
- Where funding is allocated on a competitive basis there should be procedures to ensure that it reaches the right points. Priority should be given to organisations and places that can show greatest need not to those which are good at writing bids.
- Funding application processes should be made more 'people friendly' to enable smaller community groups without the expertise of larger organisations to stand an equal chance of benefiting from grants.
- It is important to ensure that funding support for informal learning goes to where it will be properly used: to people who are actually working in the community rather than to large organisations where it may go into overheads and end up supporting not people but an infrastructure.
- Funding methodology should enable colleges to take more advantage of European funding and there should be a clearer definition of 'additionality'
- Insistence on matched funding can be a considerable drawback to widening participation as it is often difficult to obtain.

Partnerships

- Current moves towards widening participation and lifelong learning require even greater convergence of formal and non formal education to enable movement across them. It is very important for education providers to work with the voluntary sector and community groups and organisations should have equal representation in any forums or collaborative arrangements established to improve learning opportunities.
- There needs to be some articulation between the important new initiatives to widen participation. The New Deal, the Adult and Community Learning Fund, education development plans, Individual Learning Accounts and the University for Industry need to be linked into a strategic framework rather than operating in isolation from each other. Links between the Kennedy Strategic partnerships and Lifelong Learning partnerships need to be clarified.
- The current stress on partnerships can result in too many being formed, sometimes for the wrong purposes (for mercenary reasons). This can lead to a confusing plethora of *ad hoc* collaborative arrangements. There is also a danger of some partnerships being too big and unwieldy, with the result that more time and funding can be expended on the infrastructure of a partnership than on the communities it was ostensibly set up to serve. There is a need for small and clearly focused local partnerships. These should be for the benefits of learners not partners.

Guidance

- People need more than information in order to progress within education and training: they need guidance. Good quality guidance services, provided by trained staff in community settings, are essential if learners are to make informed choices on future learning paths. For many groups in the community the most effective guidance is informal and delivered face-to-face. For those without a clear idea of their future direction or without access to a telephone, helplines are not the best option.
- Initiatives to widen participation such as Individual Learning Accounts and the University

for Industry need a comprehensive guidance infrastructure in order to be fully effective. Local guidance services should include community-based organisations and voluntary sector education providers as well as formal providers. They should have accessible databases linked into local infrastructures and linked to the Learning Direct helpline. Significant assistance towards this will be made by the new funding for the development of a comprehensive local information, advice and guidance which will be linked with Learning Direct.

- 'Key' people such as local volunteers or 'learning champions' who act as 'signposters' or 'brokers' for people in their own communities can be invaluable in helping local people to know about and access local learning opportunities. Training schemes which train people in these roles should be expanded and supported.

Learner support

- Informal learning starting points for non traditional learners should be free or low cost. It is only after recognising the relevance and value of learning that many individuals are ready to invest in their own learning. However, many are then deterred by additional costs such as examination fees and travel costs. Both the Kennedy report and that of the Further Education Student Support Advisory Group Committee have observed that financial arrangements for learner support are inconsistent, inequitable and confusing. Although there have been a number of positive recent changes to help certain groups of learners, many individuals may still not be able to enter formal education for financial reasons.
- The benefit system still needs to be reformed to make it easier for unemployed people over 25 to enter or continue on a learning pathway. Although there are plans to relax the 16-hour rule and less restrictive pilot schemes have already been operating in some parts of the country, people on benefit still experience obstacles to learning.
- Funding structures should make more allowance for the support needs of non traditional learners. Those from the most disadvantaged groups need a wide range of practical and learning supports to help them move successfully along a learning pathway.

Further research

- Further research is required on the nature and scale of the impact of community-based informal learning on groups and communities. Longitudinal research in specific communities could give an idea of the overall impact.
- Research is also needed on the extent to which the skills acquired in informal learning in the community are transferable to other contexts such as the workplace, the home, voluntary work, community activism, etc.

12 Points for education and training providers arising from the study

Widening participation

- Informal programmes for learners in community settings are essential to widening participation. These can provide an effective bridge to mainstream college provision when articulated with formal programmes:

    Pre-access provision, incorporating basic skills, confidence-building and guidance, provides the essential foundation upon which long-term progression can be built. Pre-access programmes, offered locally by trained staff, give adults with few formal qualifications the confidence to return to learning and to consider more formal options thereafter. (Scottish Office, 1996: 30)

Development work

- Groundwork such as networking in the community is labour-intensive and requires considerable skills. People engaged in this capacity should not always be on short-term contracts:

    'It's not easy if you're on a temporary contract to put your heart and soul into a community and there's early burn out because of the intensity of support that's required'.
    (College outreach worker)

    The important thing is the first hook. Once you've got them through the door the possibilities are endless. It's the investment in that stage which is the most important.
    (Community education worker)

- Effective networking and outreach work in the community takes time. This should be appreciated and allowed for in work schedules, as many development workers contacted during this study stressed:

    There's no substitute for talking to people.

    You've got to spend time on the pre-figurative stuff in the community; talking to people. But no-one sees this as real work. It's too loose and unstructured, but you can't reach these people any other way.

    You could say the battle's won once you've got them through the door. It's the previous nine months that are the really hard work. Outreach work needs to be done in the pub and that often means in the evening. You need staff and resources to do this.

- Some education authorities and institutions have lost the expertise they had in dealing with local communities as a result of the policy and funding changes that came about in 1992. Appropriate staff development should be offered to staff involved in widening participation and supporting progression in community settings:

    Effective community-based provision demands a range of skills on the part of providers. These include negotiation, facilitation, appropriate teaching and learning styles, guidance, networking, development planning and financial management. While some practitioners have developed expertise in many of these areas, others have had minimal support. All staff engaged in such provision need to upgrade their skills and to learn from the expertise of colleagues from other sectors. (Scottish Office, 1996: 33)

A wide perspective and a multiplicity of skills are needed to make the links between communities and agencies and to be able to help communities develop a programme which ranges from social to economic objectives. This range of skills is unlikely to be developed in any single professional training. It spans a number of disciplines. (CLIP, 1998)

Provision
- Community-based outreach programmes should not just involve the transfer of existing programmes into the community: *'Widening participation is more than about them filling our courses. We can't expect them to just turn up and consume what we have to offer. If we just put out a course programme and wait for people to come through the door, no-one would come'* (community education worker). It is essential to consult the target groups. Non traditional learners are more likely to engage and continue in learning when they are consulted and when programmes are designed in response to their interests and needs.
- Consultation has to be real not tokenistic. It is very important for socially and economically disadvantaged groups to know that their views and preferences are listened to and respected.
- Learning starting points need to be flexible. Many people return to learning in a stereotyped areas (e.g. childcare) because it is non threatening and familiar and because they may have no idea about other learning areas. However, where people start off in learning is not necessarily where they want to go and different interests may soon emerge. A range of options need to be available to cater for emerging interests and needs.
- It is helpful to offer different kinds of provision in a community location to enable people to move between them when they are ready to do so.
- When learning needs are identified a prompt response is essential – *'getting people when they're all fired up'*. There can be too great a gap between a local needs analysis and actually setting things up. Where possible, programmes should be running at all times so that people do not have to wait for months by which time courage and momentum may have gone.
- 'Loss leaders' (free or inexpensive short courses or tasters) often lead people into longer-term learning.
- Community-based programmes should be part of the overall framework of provision and subject to the same quality assurance procedures as mainstream provision.
- Provision should be for the benefit of learners not to maximise funding for the institution.

Progression
- It is important that people who return to learn in a community environment are given the kind of support that sustains learning and are provided with a range of progression options. Foster (1997) has helpfully listed some 'principles of engagement' for working with non traditional learners:
  - Reach them where they don't feel threatened.
  - Relate to them through their interests and concerns – i.e. their young children or grandchildren, their lives and jobs.
  - Build confidence by creating supportive groups.

- Move into new knowledge and skills after raising their awareness of their existing knowledge, skills and experience.
- Open up choices and challenges on the basis of experience of success and satisfaction.
- Support them to move on not just academically but in the range of roles they are prepared to take on – as parents, as residents, as school supporters, as workers, etc.
- Help them to assess their educational and life experiences, needs and goals in defining pathway options.
- Design the timing, venue, process, activities and tutoring to reflect the needs and goals of individuals from the target group.

- An explicit policy on progression can help to focus minds on what is needed.
- Proper links with community groups and organisations should be established to assist in the creation of cross sectoral progression routes. Inter-agency links should not depend entirely on personal relationships between a few people. Stronger links between education institutions and voluntary and community groups and organisations are required to create opportunities for lifelong learning.
- It is important to recognise small steps in learning for those who are returning to education after a long gap. Individual progress, at all levels, should be recorded.
- Learner progression can be assisted by offering certificated courses but it is important to avoid introducing accreditation too soon: '*We need to know when accreditation is appropriate and beneficial, when it constrains achievement or access and when using learning outcomes and assessment to support learning is enough without a formal certificate*' (Ecclestone, 1993: 179).
- Progression is assisted when learners are offered good quality guidance throughout programmes and when they are encouraged to plan and monitor their progress through means such as action plans and records of achievement.
- Many providers are good on entry strategies but less adept at providing exit strategies. It is important to be able to point learners on to appropriate next steps at the end of a programme.
- Tracking is essential. To monitor progression, providers need to record information about earlier learning pathways, incremental learning within mainstream programmes and the destinations of learners.

Dissemination of good practice

- Good practice in community-based provision and information on progression outcomes should be shared as widely as possible through partnerships and networks.

Becoming a community resource

- If the facilities of education institutions were opened up to the wider community many more people would view education as familiar and accessible.

References

Adkins, G (1997). 'Accreditation and Progression Routes', *Adults Learning*, 8/5, January, pp 134-136

Adult Literacy and Basic Skills Unit (undated). *Progression for Basic Skills Students to Further Education and Training*

Ashton, D (1998). 'Redirecting the research agenda', in Coffield, F (ed), 1998, *Learning at Work*, ESRC Learning Society Series, Bristol, the Policy Press, pp 61-69

Baillie, S, O'Hagan, C and McAleavy, G (1998). *Bridging the Gap between Formal and Informal Learning: Accrediting prior experiential learning in higher education*, University of Ulster, Jordanstown

Ball, C (1999). 'Give students some credit', *The Times Higher*, 26 February, p 34

Batten, J, Ralph, S and Sears, M (1993). 'Communities in Crisis: an example of community-based adult education', *Adults Learning*, 4/6, February, pp 169-173

Baty, P (1999). 'Funding to raise Welsh Flexibility', *The Times Higher Education Supplement*, February 19, p 3

Baynes, P and Marks, H (1996). 'Adult Education Auxiliaries and Informal Learning' in Fieldhouse, R (ed), *A History of Modern British Adult Education*, Leicester, NIACE

BBC (1998). *Computers Don't Bite Campaign: summary of the first 13 months*, May 1997-June 1998, London, BBC

Blackwell, K (1997). *Widening Participation: bridging the learning divide*, Chesterton Community College, December

Blair, A, McPake, J and Munn, P (1993). *Facing Goliath: Adults' Experience of Participation, Guidance and Progression in Education*, SCRE Report No 46, Edinburgh, Scottish Council for Research in Education

Blythe, D (1999). 'Adult learners and OCN', *Adults Learning*, 10/5, November, pp 17-19

Brown, C (1999). 'Community Health Activists Workington South (CHAWS)', in WEA, *Best Practice: effective teaching and learning in WEA courses and projects*, WEA, London, p 31

Brown, J (1999). 'Looking for Guidance?' *Adults Learning*, 10/7, February, pp 6-7

Butterworth, C (1992). 'More than one bite at the APEL', *Journal of Further and Higher Education*, 16/3, p 39-51

Campaign for Learning/MORI (1998). *Attitudes to learning*

Capizzi, E (1999). *Learning that works: accrediting the TUC Programme*, TUC/NIACE

Caudry, A (1985). 'Community tussles 'twixt tweeds and leathers', *Times Educational Supplement*, 5 April, p 10

Channel Four Television (1995). *Consenting Adults: Making the most of mentoring*, London, Channel Four

Charnley, AH, Osborn, M, Withnall, A (1981). *The Voluntary Field, Review of Existing Research in Adult and Continuing Education*, vol V, Leicester, NIACE

Charnley, AH, Osborn, M, Withnall, A (1983). *Adult Education and the Local Community, Review of Existing Research in Adult and Continuing Education*, vol X11, Leicester, NIACE

Chew, C and Platten, J (1998). 'Upstairs-Downstairs', *Adults Learning*, 10/12, pp 6-8

City of Coventry Community Education Service (undated). *The CEALE Report: the Community Education and Local Enterprise Project*, Coventry

Coalfields Learning Initiatives Partnership (CLIP) (1998). *The Critical Contribution of Learning in the Regeneration of Post-Industrial Communities*, CLIP, Northern College, Barnsley

Coffield, F (ed) (1998). *Learning at Work*, ESRC Learning Society Series, Bristol, The Policy Press

Cordon, R (1993). *Where next? Progression routes for adult learners*, WEA Cheshire, Merseyside and West Lancashire District, Liverpool

CRAC/NICEC (1998). *Individual Learning Accounts: the role of information advice and Guidance*, Report on a NICEC/ CRAC policy consultation held on 4-5 June 1998 at the Belmont Hotel, Leicester, in association with the National Advisory Council for Careers and Educational Guidance

Crequer, N (1999). 'Capital courses in state of chaos', *Times Educational Supplement*, 12 March, p 30

DfEE (1998a). *The Learning Age: A Renaissance for a New Britain*, London, The Stationery Office

DfEE (1998b). *Local Information and Advice and Guidance for adults in England Towards a National Framework*, Sheffield, DfEE

DfEE (1998c). *Arrangements for Effective Student Support in Further Education*, Report of the Further Education Student Support Advisory Group

DfEE (1999). *Local Information and Advice and Guidance for adults in England: Towards a national framework*

Donnelly, C (1997). 'Students and Colleges frustrated by 21-hour rule', *Working Brief*, March, pp 10-14

Duke, C (1995). 'Formal Systems: working from within' in Mayo, M and Thomson J (eds) *Adult Learning, Critical Intelligence and Social Change*, Leicester, NIACE, pp 253-261

Ecclestone, K (1993). 'Accreditation in adult learning: how far can we go?' *Adults Learning*, 4/7, pp 178-180

Elsdon, K with Reynolds, J and Stewart, S (1995). *Voluntary Organisations: Citizenship, learning and change*, Leicester, NIACE

Elsey, B (1974). 'Voluntary Organisations and Informal Adult learning', *Adult Education*, 46/6, March, pp 391-396

Eraut, M (1997). *Perspectives on defining 'The Learning Society'*. Paper prepared for the ESRC Learning Society Programme. Brighton, Institute of Education, University of Sussex

Eraut, M, Alderton, J, Cole, G and Senker, P (1998). *Development of Knowledge and Skills in Employment*, Research Report No 5, University of Sussex, Institute of Education

Fazaeli, T (1991). *Innovations in Access 2: Case Studies*, Leicester, UDACE

Field, J (1998). 'The Silent Explosion – living in the learning society', *Adults Learning*, 10/4, December, pp 6-8

Foley, G (1999). *Learning in Social Action: a contribution to understanding informal education*, Leicester, NIACE

Fordham, P (1979). 'The Interaction of Formal and non formal Education', *Studies in Adult Education*, 11/1, pp 1-11

Foster, P (1997). *Review of ParentScope Initiative within Birmingham LEA*, London, FEDA

Foster, P, Howard, U and Reisenberger, A (1997). 'A Sense of Achievement: Outcomes of adult learning', *FE Matters*, 2/3, London, Further Education Development Agency

Fraser, W (1995). 'Making Experience Count...Towards What?', in Mayo, M and Thompson J (eds), *Adult Learning, Critical Intelligence and Social Change*, Leicester, NIACE, pp 137-145

Fryer, RH (1997). *Learning for the 21st Century. First Report of the National Advisory Group for Continuing Education and Lifelong Learning*, HMSO

Further Education Unit (1993). *Open College Networks: Participation and progression*, London, FEU

Further Education Development Agency (1995). *Progression for Adult Learners from Informal to Qualification-bearing courses*, London, Further Education Development Agency

Further Education Development Agency (1997). 'A sense of achievement: outcomes of adult learning', *FE Matters*, 2/3

Gurnah, A (1997). *A New Funding Framework for Adult Education*, RaPAL Bulletin No 34, Spring, pp 15-18

Hamilton, M (date). 'Literacy and Adult Basic Education', in Fieldhouse, R and Associates, *A History of Modern British Adult Education*, pp 142-165

Hargreaves (1985). In Ranson, S and Tomlinson, J (eds), *The Government of Education*, George Allen and Unwin

Harre Hindmarsh, J and Davies, L (1995). *Adults' Learning Pathways: a pilot study in the Wellington Region*, Victoria University of Wellington, Department of Education

Higher Education Funding Council England (1998). *Good Practice in Non Award-Bearing Continuing Education*, 98/49, Bristol, HEFCE

The Home Office Voluntary and Community Sector Working Group on Government Relations (1998). *Compact: getting it right together: compact on relations between Government and the Voluntary and Community Sector in England*, London, the Home Office

Jackson, K (1995). 'Popular Education and the State: a new look at the community debate', in Mayo, M and Thompson, J (eds), *Adult Learning, Critical Intelligence and Social Change*, Leicester, NIACE,
pp 182-203

Jessup, G (1995). In Burke, J (ed), *Outcomes, learning and the curriculum*, Falmer Press

Kendall, J and Knapp, M (1993). *Defining the non-profit sector: the United Kingdom*, Working papers of the John Hopkins Comparative Non Profit Sector Project, University of Kent and Canterbury

Kirkwood, C (1978). 'Adult Education and the Concept of Community', *Adult Education*, 5/1, pp 145-151

Lovett, T, Clarke, C and Kilmurray, A (1983). *Adult Education and Community Action*, Croom Helm

Lynn, P and Davis Smith, J (1991). *The 1991 National Survey of Voluntary Activity in the UK*, London, The Volunteer Centre UK

Macfarlane, R (1997). *Unshackling the Poor: a complementary approach, to local economic development*, Joseph Rowntree Foundation, York Publishing Services Ltd

Mager, C (1993). 'Progression from LEA to College Provision: the role of Open College Networks', *Adults Learning*, 4/5, January

Martin, I (1987). 'Community Education: towards a theoretical analysis', in Allen, G, Bastiani, J, Martin, L and Richards, K (eds), *Community Education: an agenda for educational reform*, Open University Press, pp 9-31

Maxwell, B (1997). *Realising the Potential of Community Education*, MEd thesis (unpublished), University of Wales, Bangor

McGivney, V (1990). *Evaluation of the Women's Education Project in Belfast*, Belfast, Women's Education Project/ Leicester, NIACE

——— (1992). *Tracking Adult Learning Routes: pilot investigation into adult learners' starting points and progression to further education and training*, Leicester, NIACE

——— (1994). *Adult Learning Pathways: a case study in the Taff Ely district*, Cardiff, NIACE CYMRU

——— (1996). *Staying or leaving the course: non-completion and retention of mature students in further and higher education*, Leicester, NIACE

——— (1998a). *Final evaluation of Gloucester Primary Health Project*, unpublished, GLOSCAT, Gloucester

——— (1998b). *Adults Learning in Pre-Schools*, Leicester, NIACE

——— (1999). *Excluded Men: men who are missing from education and training*, Leicester, NIACE

McGivney, V and Thomson, A (1995). *Foundation Training: responding to labour market change*, a report commissioned by Coventry City Council City Development Directorate, Coventry City Council Economic Development Division

McIntyre, J and Kimberley, H (1998). *Planning Pathways for Women from Adult Community Education to Vocational Education and Training*, project report, Research Centre for Vocational Education and Training, University of Technology, Sydney

McNair, S with Cara, S, McGivney, V, Raybould, F, Soulsby, J, Thomson, T, Vaughan, M (1999). *Non Award-Bearing Continuing Education: an evaluation of the HEFCE programme 1995-1998*, HEFCE, Bristol

Merton, B (1998). *Only Connect*, Leicester, NIACE

Munn, P, Tett, L and Arney, N (1993). *Negotiating the Labyrinth: progression opportunities for adult learner*, SCRE Report No 47, Edinburgh, the Scottish Council for Research in Education

National Credit Framework Strategic Advisory Group (1998). *Qualifying for Success: on Unitisation and Credit : A joint statement*

NIACE (1998). *A review of Adult Learners' Week 16-22 May 1998*, Leicester, NIACE

NICEC (1998). *Adult Guidance in Community Settings*, Briefing paper by the National Institute for Careers Education and Counselling, Cambridge, NICEC

National Open College Network (1998). *OCNs and Access to Higher Education: update* – a guide for HE admissions staff

Nolan, P, Field, J, Francis, H, Gale, P, Stokes, G (1998). *Building Democracy: Community, Citizenship and Civil Society*, a paper for the National Advisory Group on Continuing Education and Lifelong Learning

Percy, K with Barnes, B, Graddon, A and Machell, J (1988). *Learning in Voluntary Organisations*, Leicester, UDACE

Percy, K and Ward, P (1991). *The Progress of Unemployed Adults in Three Open Colleges*, Final report of FEU REPLAN Project RP 464, London, Further Education Unit, unpublished

Rees, G, Fevre, R, Furlong, J, Gorard, S (1997). 'History, Place and the Learning Society: towards a sociology of lifelong learning', *Journal of Education Policy*, 12/6, pp 485-497

Salamon, LM and Anheier, HK (1993). 'Comparative study of the non profit sector: methodology, definition and classification', in Saxon-Harrold, SE and Kendall, J (eds), *Researching the Voluntary Sector*, Tonbridge, Charities Aid Foundation, pp 179-196

Scottish Council for Research in Education (SCRE) (1993). *Facing Goliath: adults' experiences of participation, guidance and progression in education*

——— *Negotiating the labyrinth*

——— *Where do we go from Here? Adult educational guidance in Scotland*

The Scottish Office (1996). *Lifelong Learning in the Community*, Liaise (Learning Initiatives for Adults in Scottish Education), Education and Industry Department the Scottish Office

Scribbens, J and Howard, U (eds) (1998). 'ILT and Lifelong Learning: a strategic view', in *College Research: a journal for further education and lifelong learning*, Summer, pp 6-8

The Social Exclusion Unit (1998). *Bringing People Together: a national strategy for neighbourhood renewal*

Simkins, T (1977). *Non-formal Education and Development*, University of Manchester, quoted in Fordham, 1977, *op cit*

Stamper, A (1998). *Rooms off the Corridor: Education in the WI and 50 Years of Denman College, 1948-1998*, Leicester, NIACE/London, WI Books

Temple, J (1991). *Age of Opportunity? Progression routes and outcomes for students in Adult Basic Education from Hackney Adult Education Institute and Hackney Reading Centre*, ALFA, London, North and East London Open College Network

Trades Union Congress (1998). *Union Gateway to Learning*, TUC Learning Services Report

Universities' Association for Continuing Education (UACE) (1995). *University Continuing Education with the Minority Ethnic Communities*, Universities Association for Continuing Education, May

Unit for the Development of Adult Continuing Education (UDACE) (1987). *Understanding Each Other: voluntary/statutory relationships in the education of adults*, Leicester, UDACE

——— (1988a). *Working Together: developing voluntary/statutory collaboration and adult learning: the policy paper*, Leicester, UDACE

——— (1988b). *Developing Access: a development paper*, Leicester, UDACE

Ward, J (1998). 'Creating Role Models, Adults: increasing the participation of adult Asian learners on Access courses', *Adults Learning*, 10/1, September, pp 24-26

Weller, P (1993). 'Community Education in a Credit Union', *Adults Learning*, 44/5, 1993, pp 130-131

The Widening Participation Committee (1997). *New Learning Pathway: accreditation of guidance and tutorial support*, consultation paper

Wilson, P (1997). *New Learning Pathways: accreditation of guidance and tutorial support*, Leicester, NIACE

Winkless, C (1999). *Fees Survey 1997-98: Indicators of fee levels charged to part-time students by Local Education Authorities and Colleges*, Leicester, NIACE

Workers' Educational Association (The National Association) (1997a). *Cutting Edges IV: Innovation and new directions in the educational provision of the Workers Educational Association*, WEA Development Fund Reports 1996/97, London, WEA the National Association

——— (1997b). *Educational Guidance*, WEA Development Fund Report, London, WEA the National Association

——— (1998a). *Bringing down the barriers: first WEA submission to the Learning Age Consultation*, London, WEA the National Association

——— (1998b). *Realising the Vision: Second WEA submission to the Learning Age Consultation*, London, WEA the National Association

Some examples of progression routes from Open College Network-accredited programmes within the Open College Network Centre, England

Organisation	OCN Programme	Level	Number of Learners since programme recognised	Profile of Learners	Progression Routes
A.C.E Health Project South Warwickshire Health Promotion Service	Health and personal development	1, 2	12-16 per course	Women, disabled women	In one course with 12 participants: 2 to full-time employment, 1 to Access to HE course, 1 to other accredited training course (30% to employment and other education/ training)
The Lighthouse, Coventry	Christian Counselling	2, 3	32	Adults	All have become counsellors in the voluntary sector; 3 have gone on to other courses and 10 are planning to
Community Works, Redditch	Courses on "Making Communities work"	Entry 1, 2, 3	450	Adult returners seeking new life/work options	Full-time employment 10%, Part-time employment: 8%, Other OCN courses: 15%, FE courses: 7%, HE programmes: 1%
Coventry Muslim Community Association Ltd	Techniques of Sewing; Asian Fashion Design	1, 2, 3	200+	Women seeking new life/work options	About 25% have progressed to: – City and Guilds levels 1-2, BTEC Nursery Nursing, Jobs in clothing and textile industry, Computer Courses
British Institute of Learning Disabilities (BILD)	Courses for care staff	2, 3	4	Care Staff	2 have progressed to NVQ levels 2 and 3
Churches Initiative on Training, Employment and Enterprise (CITEE)	Return to learn or work; "A Foot in the Door"	1, 2	52	Long-term unemployed, recovering people mentally ill, with health and other problems	12 have progressed to employment, further education and voluntary work
National Federation of Young Farmers	Personal development, farm experience programme, life skills	1, 2, 3	640	Young farmers	NVQ (4%)
Stoke Park School & Community College	Mental Health Awareness	1,2	20	Carers, survivors of mental health system, community providers in mental health field	4 have moved into other courses at Stoke Park: Psychology, Counselling and Turkish
Stoke Park School & Community College	Reflexology	1,2	Not given	Interested persons	2 into Reflexology diploma programme, 2 into other courses
Stoke Park School & Community College	Extending Essential Skills	Entry to level 2	200	People needing help with basic skills	between 50 and 75 have moved to a range of other courses including Maths Workshop, Computer Workshop, Childcare, Key Skills
Stoke Park School & Community College	Aromatherapy and Massage	1,2	Not given	Mature students	70% of learners go onto diploma and other higher level programmes